What people are saying about …

He Is My Life

"A Bible study that can bring the brokenhearted to the Great Healer."

Francine Rivers, author of *Redeeming Love*

"Debbie Alsdorf's studies will help you affirm your identity, renew your hope, redefine your purpose, and know God as Deliverer!"

Carol Kent, speaker and author of *When I Lay My Isaac Down*

"I love when I find Truth with a capital T! Debbie Alsdorf offers profound concepts in simple, easy-to-apply ways. These are the perfect Bible studies for women who've just met the Savior, or for those of us who are ready to take our relationship with Him to the next level."

Liz Curtis Higgs, best-selling author of *Bad Girls of the Bible*

"Jesus said that He came to give life and give it abundantly. Debbie does a beautiful job facilitating this truth through her book. Read it and be blessed!"

Denalyn and Max Lucado

DESIGN {4} LIVING

HE IS MY Life

Living to Love
Others as Jesus Did

DEBBIE ALSDORF

David C Cook®
transforming lives together

HE IS MY LIFE
Published by David C. Cook
4050 Lee Vance View
Colorado Springs, CO 80918 U.S.A.

David C. Cook Distribution Canada
55 Woodslee Avenue, Paris, Ontario, Canada N3L 3E5

David C. Cook U.K., Kingsway Communications
Eastbourne, East Sussex BN23 6NT, England

David C. Cook and the graphic circle C logo
are registered trademarks of Cook Communications Ministries.

The Web site addresses recommended throughout this book are offered as a resource to you. These Web sites are not
intended in any way to be or imply an endorsement on the part of David C. Cook, nor do we vouch for their content.

Unless otherwise noted, all Scripture references are taken from the *Holy Bible, New International Version® NIV®*.
Copyright © 1973, 1978, 1984 by International Bible Society. Used by permission of Zondervan. All rights reserved.
Additional Scripture taken from *The Amplified Bible* (AB), Copyright © 1954, 1958, 1962, 1964, 1965, 1987
by The Lockman Foundation. Used by permission; *THE MESSAGE* (MSG). Copyright © by Eugene Peterson
1993, 1994, 1995, 1996, 2000, 2001, 2002. Used by permission of NavPress Publishing Group; the *Holy
Bible, New Living Translation*, copyright © 1996. Used by permission of Tyndale House Publishers, Inc.,
Wheaton, Illinois 60189. All rights reserved; the King James Version of the Bible (KJV). (Public Domain.)
Italics in Scripture are added by the author for emphasis.

ISBN 978-1-4347-6788-2

© 2008 Debbie Alsdorf
Previously published in 2000 by Faithful Woman as *Living Love* by Debbie Alsdorf. ISBN 0-7814-3383-5.

The Team: Terry Behimer, Karen Lee-Thorp, Amy Kiechlin, Jaci Schneider, and Susan Vannaman
Cover/Interior Design: ThinkPen Design, Greg Jackson
Cover Photo: © Richard Seagraves, Workbook Stock, Jupiter Images

Printed in the United States of America
Second Edition 2008

1 2 3 4 5 6 7 8 9 10

090308

Dedicated to
my sons, Justin and Cameron Brier.
It is because of my love for you that I made the choice
to learn what it really means to live in God's love.
Though I am still learning, it is my prayer that what has
been planted in your hearts will make a difference in
your relationship with God and with others.

These commandments that I give you today
are to be upon your hearts.
Impress them on your children.

—DEUTERONOMY 6:6–7

So the next generation would know them,
even the children yet to be born,
and they in turn would tell their children.

—PSALM 78:6

My command is this: Love each other as I have loved you.

—JOHN 15:12

CONTENTS

ACKNOWLEDGMENTS

It is in the context of relationships that we learn how to live in God's love. I would like to thank the following people for their influence in my life.

Ray … my husband and my friend. You are a true example of putting others first. May we spend our days learning what it means to live in God's love. You are a gift, and I love you (Rom. 8:28).

Pauline Davis … a precious neighbor from Chewacan Drive. You taught me how to reach out with God's love. The boys and I will never forget how you loved us in practical ways.

Julie Fox … my friend who walks the practical side of love. Your cards, calls, and friendship over the years mean so much to me.

Grace King … your hugs every Sunday morning as I enter Cornerstone are like an embrace from heaven. You are a wonderful example to me of God's love in action.

Kim Dunn … you are truly a sunshine girl and an example of God's kindness and love in action. Your life refreshes many.

Christy Harper … you encourage so many women to BE like Jesus. Your example of faithfulness encourages me.

Pastors Steve Madsen, Mark Calcagno, and Bob Ferro … you have been an example to me of people who seek to live the love of God. Thank you for your encouragement. It has been healing.

The women of Cornerstone Fellowship … because of you, I am daily learning more about walking the walk of love. Together may we continue to desire God's heart—forgiving, loving, and accepting one another. We are all in process.

It is my prayer that Jesus will be our life, our example, and the heartbeat of who we are.

INTRODUCTION

This Bible study is intended to promote real-life change in the way we live life with other people. We will see through the study of God's Word how we can

- forgive those who have hurt us;
- accept those who disapprove of us;
- handle hurt in a new and productive way;
- learn that conflict is a fact of life, but drama is optional;
- experience the joy of being God's vessel of love to others.

God loves each of us with an extravagant love. His love goes beyond our mistakes and shortcomings. His love goes beyond our personality quirks, bad days, and bad attitudes. It is wonderful when we begin to understand God's love for us personally. But we can't stop there—God desires to fill us with His love and teach us what it means to love others. When Christ becomes our life, His love becomes our example, and His way of relating becomes our goal.

We have been created for relationship—relationship with God and with one another. In this life one thing is clear—God calls us to love one another. But we often don't take the call to love others seriously. We add conditions to His command, supposing that we have a menu of different options depending on our present circumstances or the dynamics of our current relationships. We pick and choose whom to love, whom to forgive, and whom to reach out to. Our choice is often based on our own feelings of hurt or the past baggage that we bring into our Christian walk. Women have even been known to blame their poor relational actions on their hormones—month after month. Unfortunately, even though we love God and want to follow His way, our relationships and our actions often don't line up to the standard of His love.

I have often thought that I could learn to live in God's love if I were living alone on a mountaintop or tucked away in a cave. There in the quietness and peace of not having to deal with other people, I could think about God's love and come up with a great plan. In that place of seclusion, I could love everybody and everything. There would be nothing to stop me from love—no disappointments, no disagreements, and no conflict. Can you relate?

The challenge is the fact that we aren't living on a mountaintop or in the seclusion of a cave. We are living in homes with people who rub us the wrong way, say the wrong things, and often take us for granted. We are working in offices with people of different interests, different backgrounds, and different personalities. Add to the mix all the complex relationships of today—in-laws, out-laws, and ex-laws—and you have a real problem on your hands. I think we could all agree that it's easy to love those who behave the way we would like them to, but in real life we often live in the battlefield of misunderstandings.

I have had my share of challenging relationships. I have lived the past eighteen years in the whirling blades of the blended family. We have four kids—two of his, two of mine—and a mix of in-laws, out-laws, and ex-laws. I have also been in ministry for many years and know about those who are for you, those who are against you, and those who are just watching you. Yes, I know about the challenge of relationships. But, I also know the joy of learning what it means to live beyond ourselves and in the fullness of God's love in each difficult circumstance and relationship we face.

When my children were young, I realized that I could never teach them about Jesus and His love while living in bitterness toward others. It made little sense to speak to them of God's love while holding tightly to resentments, grudges, and bitterness. My relationships weren't perfect, so I had a dilemma. I had to decide which direction I would set my heart and my life toward. God gave me the grace and strength to choose life through His Word instead of choosing spiritual, emotional, and relational death by living according to my selfishness. Did I gravitate toward selfishness? As I am human, of course my natural bent is toward my selfish nature. But I began to experience a different kind of life when I took God's call to live in His love seriously. The exciting part is that He provides everything we need to live in His love.

Each day I am aware that He continually gives me the grace to choose His love over the alternative. God will give you the grace to live in His love too. It is in this place that we become free—no longer bound by expectations of how people should treat us but free to live in submission to the Father's will, which is to "love each other" (John 15:17). Jesus told us to remain in His love so that His joy would be in us and our joy would be complete (John 15:10–11).

Daily we have choices. Living in love is a choice. Your choice to follow after the heart and will of God is simply the starting point. At times it is the most difficult choice you will make—a lip-biting, teeth-grinding choice. The power for change doesn't come by your choice, but the change comes by the power of God's Spirit working on your heart. Though your choice is important in pointing you in the right direction, it is the power of God that will change you from the inside out.

This study isn't about living nicely or perfectly in all relationships. It is about pointing your heart in the right direction, and allowing the Word of God to be a compass that will direct your life and your interactions with other people. In this study we will be focusing on what the Bible says about how to live toward other people. You will be looking at Scripture to direct you in your everyday relationships.

We will look at the red letters of Christ's words and learn from His example. We will see relevance in Scripture as we find answers to some of the most practical questions, such as:

- How, as a Christian, do I balance my feelings with my faith?
- Is living in God's love just learning to be nice?
- How do I love those who have hurt me?
- What is forgiveness, and how do I live in it?
- How do I handle conflict and still honor God in my relationships?
- What is it about me that resists reaching out to others?
- Does God expect me to love people I have no interest in?
- How do I walk in love despite my moods and attitudes?

You can do this study individually, with a friend, or in a group. Always begin by praying for understanding, asking the Holy Spirit to lead you into the truth of God's way for you. If you do this study in a group, I suggest you work through one lesson a week. Each lesson has five days of personal study, a journaling exercise, and daily prayer. You will need a Bible, a dictionary, and a thesaurus—and time set apart for sitting with the truths of Scripture. You may also want to purchase a separate journal for recording the things you are learning as you study.

Sometimes you will spend a considerable amount of time with one passage of Scripture. Sometimes you will come back to the same passage more than once. The purpose of returning to a passage is to meditate on it so that it sinks into your heart.

Also, you will often be asked to write out whole verses. I find that the act of writing the words helps me think about each one. I hear the verses better, and I remember them better. Don't think of this as mere busy work—it's another way of meditating on the verse.

Jesus Christ has the wonderful ability to change us from the inside out. He can heal our hearts, heal relationships, and pick us up where we have fallen down. Together let's set our hearts toward God, making the choice to walk the walk and not just talk the talk. Let's step into freedom as we learn to live and love God's way. It is a happier and more peaceful way to live. After all, if Christ is our life, shouldn't He be our example in the most practical areas of living?

Learning to walk in God's love,
Debbie Alsdorf

DESIGN: A PLAN, INTENT, OR A PURPOSE.

Every Design4Living resource is developed to draw women closer to Christ and to encourage intimacy between a woman and her Maker. Design4Living is dedicated to helping women line up to the truth of God's Word in the practical places of everyday life. Life change and real transformation comes when a woman's mind is renewed by the truth in God's Word. When a woman knows the truth, she is set free to live a different life—a life designed for her by God.

4 ways to love God (Mark 12:30)
- Heart
- Soul
- Strength
- Mind

4 truths to build a foundation of stability and peace (Ps. 139)
- He Knows Me
- He Protects Me
- He Created Me
- He Values Me

4 beliefs that simplify a woman's life (Col. 1:16, Matt. 22:37–40)
- I have been Created *by* God
- I have been Created *for* God
- I have been Created to Love God
- I have been Created to Love Others

Daily Prayer

So far today, God,
I've done all right …
I haven't gossiped.
I haven't been grumpy, nasty or selfish.
I'm really glad of that,
but in a few minutes, God,
I'm going to get out of bed.
From now on, I'm probably going to need a lot of help.[1]

Living Love ... In Our Daily Choices

LESSON 1

He who believes in Me—out of his heart will flow rivers of living water—and hundreds of other lives will be continually refreshed. Now is the time for us to break "the flask" of our lives, to stop seeking our own satisfaction, and to pour out our lives before Him.

—OSWALD CHAMBERS

Love is one of the few things in life worth pursuing with a godly passion. But loving others is one of the hardest things in life unless all conditions are just right—then, maybe then, we are willing to let go and love. The reality is that Christians don't love automatically. It is a fact that we are ordinary people—human beings with fleshly tendencies. But many of us think that love should flow out of our every pore once we have committed our lives to Christ. Unfortunately, there is no automatic love switch that flips on when we come to Christ. We come to Christ just as the human flesh we are—no more, no less. And as we surrender our lives and our wills to Him, things in our lives begin to take a different shape. It is a process.

God's love is like a key that has been expressly designed to unlock our hearts and the hearts of those we love. Many of us are locked up inside. We are hurting, frustrated, and confused. We need the touch of God's love, because His love is the key to salvation, fulfillment, and relationship with Him. Our relationships can be rewarding, or they can be a disastrous set of unmet expectations. The first step in loving others is understanding God's love for us personally. When God's love for us becomes a core belief and a living reality, it changes the way we look at ourselves and at our lives. It also changes how we look at other people.

From the beginning of time God has created us for relationship with Himself and relationship with each other—but things have gotten in the way. It started with Adam and Eve in that beautiful

Garden of Eden. Pride got in the way; they did their own thing and disobeyed God. Then they blamed each other and ultimately hid from God. Sometimes we aren't much different! Like Eve we take the bait, make a selfish choice, blame everyone else, and then hide from God and others as our relationships crumble around our feet. Thankfully, God in His love sent the answer by sending His Son Jesus. From the point of salvation until the day we take our last breath, each of us needs the power of God to live in the rich, full life that has been designed for us from the beginning of time—a life of relationship with God and others.

We must always keep in mind that it is His love, given by His Spirit, that is the key. No amount of love we could muster up in our own strength will unlock the doors to lasting fulfillment in relationships with others. It is God's love that has the power to change our lives and the lives of those we come in contact with. *My ability to love others is directly related to the condition of my own heart before God.*

Spiritual growth does not happen overnight. In the same way, learning to relate to others God's way is a process of growth and surrender. Loving God's way is the process of recognizing our value to God and in turn recognizing the value of others. When we begin to understand the value God assigns to each person in our life's path, we will have a decision to make—to agree with the value God assigns and treat others the way Jesus would or ignore the value God assigns and treat others the way we feel like we want to. The choice is ours to make, but the choice that changes us is the one that lines up with the truth of God's Word. Jesus loves people and He is our example.

Why is the choice to love so hard? Hurts, misunderstandings, unmet expectations, and personal insecurities are probably the biggest culprits of bad relationships. When we are insecure others easily threaten us. In this place it is hard to honestly esteem others with the significance and value they deserve as God's own beloved children. Women in record numbers suffer with insecurities and low self-esteem. Even within churches, women silently suffer with feelings of being less than enough. But when a woman begins to grasp God's great love for her, and that reality goes from head knowledge to the heartbeat of who she is, she will become convinced that she should honor others with that same wonderful love.

If you are struggling with insecure thoughts and feelings of worthlessness, you need to spend some time soaking in God's love for you. Allowing the truth in God's Word to penetrate those insecurities will be the first step in personal wholeness and stability. Think about what God's Word says to you individually. The first study book in the Design4Living series, *He Is My All: Living in the Truth of God's*

Love for Me, would be helpful to lay a foundation for you, or encouraging as a refresher helping with internalizing the truth of God's love for you. Internalizing the truth of God's love is a good starting point toward replacing low self-esteem and insecurity with peace and confidence. As you fill yourself with God's Word and His thoughts toward you, you will become more equipped for loving others because you will understand the very nature of God's love.

Let's begin our study together—we have a lot of ground to cover.

 DAY ONE: THE HOPE OF A NEW LOVE TO LIVE BY

1. Read Matthew 16:13–19.

In verse 15, Jesus asks who Peter thinks He is. This question is just as appropriate for us today. People hold so many different opinions about Jesus. Nearly all world religions acknowledge Him, but not all religions acknowledge that He is the Messiah or the Son of God. Many don't realize that He is still alive. Christian faith is based on the death and resurrection of Jesus Christ. Christians believe in a *living God*. It is because He lives that we can face any relationship, any challenge, any insult.

• Is your relationship with God alive? How do you know?

• Do you believe in a living God? Why, or why not?

• What was Jesus' response to Simon Peter's answer (Matt. 16:17)?

• According to this passage, who reveals to our hearts the reality of who Jesus Christ is? Why does that matter?

(If you are still uncertain about who Jesus really is, ask God to show you.)

• What did Jesus say He would give Simon Peter?

Some people use this verse to claim all kinds of things that God never claimed would be unlocked for them. Naming and claiming can leave us confused and disappointed if what we are naming and claiming is not God's will for us. But we can safely say that living in God's love is definitely God's will for us. He gives us the keys of love, the keys of His kingdom, so that His character might be unlocked in us. It is by the love of God that we can become content, joyful women who are filled with hope and security.

It is God's love that will
set us apart for His purposes
and
set us free to love others.

Everything that pertains to life was given to God's Son, and now He gives it all to us. As Jesus walked on this earth, the love of the Father filled Him. It was no ordinary love that gave Jesus the courage to go to the cross. It was the extraordinary love of the Father that compelled Him to commit His life to the will and plan of God. This same love compels us to give our all to Jesus. No other love will be sufficient for the tasks that He has planned for us. No other love will withstand insult and injury. No other love will give us the capacity for forgiveness. Nothing but the love of God will enable us to go the extra mile!

Pray that this love of God will be unlocked and poured out in your everyday life. His love let loose on earth through you is an exhilarating experience. Seek God for His love and seek to be a vessel of that love. A vessel of love is simply a woman God will flow through to love others. As we are filled up with Christ, we can be poured out for others. In this way, we can be God's instruments of love and peace. People moving with the heartbeat of God.

God's love is the key. And His Spirit is the locksmith, waiting to dispense to you what is needed to open the hearts of the people God has placed in your life. Over the next several weeks we will be looking at three different things:

> This is the rock on which I will put together my church, a church so expansive with energy that not even the gates of hell will be able to keep it out. And that's not all. You will have complete and free access to God's kingdom, keys to open any and every door: no more barriers between heaven and earth, earth and heaven (Matt. 16:18–19 MSG).

1. What is God's love, and how does it differ from human love?
2. What does it mean to love God with all of our heart, will, and soul?
3. What does it mean to love our neighbor as ourselves?

We are not going to learn techniques or methods to learn to love like God. We cannot learn to do what only God can do. What we will learn is

- the importance of yielding ourselves to God, thus making better choices;
- how to choose to set aside our own thoughts, emotions, and desires that are contrary to God's, so He then will show His love through us.

We can't change our pasts, and we can't make everything in our lives turn out the way we want. We certainly can't change other people, and we can't control circumstances where other people's choices are involved. But we can

- keep our eyes focused on Jesus;
- yield ourselves totally to Him;
- allow His love to flood our souls and overflow into all or our experiences each day.

We must pray and ask that the love of God would be evident in our lives, and that His love would actually love others through us—through our touch, our words, our smile, our actions, and so on. The people

> I will give you the keys of the kingdom of heaven; and whatever you bind [declare to be improper and unlawful] on earth must be what is already bound in heaven; and whatever you loose [declare lawful] on earth must be what is already loosed in heaven (Matt. 16:19 AB).

in our lives better fasten their seat belts, because by the power of God's Spirit, love is coming their way! It is my prayer that you will become convinced through the evidence in God's Word that walking in love is exactly the path He intends for you. It will take you a step toward unbroken communion with the Father. As you step closer to this type of relationship, you will begin moving in the ways of the Spirit. Love will be the by-product of your personal interaction with Christ.

2. Read Romans 5:5–8

• What has God poured into our hearts?

• How can we be sure God loves us?

• Write out Romans 5:5 and memorize this verse. It is important to remember that the source of love is always God and not yourself or others!

Such hope never disappoints or deludes or shames us, for God's love has been poured out in our hearts through the Holy Spirit Who has been given to us (Rom. 5:5 AB).

The Word of God clearly tells us that God has poured His love into our hearts by the Holy Spirit (Rom. 5:5). We can do nothing of eternal value without being connected to our heavenly Father. The choice then that counts is the choice to live connected to the Father—abiding and remaining in Him. This is the key. In desiring to live God's love toward others, it is very important never to lose sight of this foundational truth. We want to love, but sometimes people are unloving, difficult, obnoxious, or hurtful. There are other times when we really want to love, but we are hurting, needy, or just too tired to be bothered with thinking of everyone else. This is exactly why we need to rely on a fresh flow of God's love into our hearts and lives each day. It must be His love that flows through us. When it is His love working in us and through us, we can move through life, learning to love despite others' responses or our own current emotional energy level.

3. Read Hosea 2:7–20.

In this passage we see Hosea's love for his unfaithful wife, Gomer. Her unfaithfulness is a picture of Israel's unfaithfulness in her relationship with God. Instead of responding to God in thankfulness and love, the Israelites offered what they had to idols. They went after things and people to find love and fulfillment, instead of being thankful for God and His love.

> We're never left feeling shortchanged. Quite the contrary—we can't round up enough containers to hold everything God generously pours into our lives through the Holy Spirit! (Rom. 5:5 MSG).

• According to Hosea 2:8 and 2:13, whom did Israel forget?

• Maybe you have a habit of forgetting God. Have you ever experienced God drawing you back to Himself as He did here with Israel? (See 2:14.) If so, describe your experience.

• Write out Hosea 2:19–20.

Betroth comes from a Hebrew word that means pledged or pledged to be married.[1] It is not a word that we use much today, but being pledged to another person through the covenant of marriage is still significant. We would probably say engaged instead of betrothed, but the meaning remains the same.

• What does this Hosea passage say to you personally when you stop and think of God pledging Himself to you and you to Him forever?

- Think of what it means to be engaged to someone. It is a connection, an interlocking, a tie-in with someone, a connection of two hearts—a commitment to travel through life together. How is this like the kind of connection God wants with us?

- Instead of forgetting the Lord and His love, what does this passage say you could do?

- Who or what holds the key to your heart today? (Consider things, people, agendas, or your dreams.)

- Have your own feelings of hurt or misunderstanding become your personal idols? If so, how?

- Can you trust in the Lord enough just for today to give Him the set of keys that you have and ask only, "Thy will be done"? What would that involve?

I will betroth you to Me forever; yes, I will betroth you to Me in righteousness and justice, in steadfast love, and in mercy. I will even betroth you to Me in stability and in faithfulness, and you shall know [recognize, be acquainted with, appreciate, give heed to and cherish] the Lord (Hos. 2:19–20 AB).

4. Look up and record the dictionary definition of *acknowledge*.

Write out "I will acknowledge the Lord" (based on Hos. 2:20) on a 3 x 5 card and carry it with you as a bookmark. Or put it on your car dash, or tape it to your mirror, or put it somewhere on your office desk. Let this card serve as a reminder to always acknowledge (recognize, be acquainted with, appreciate, give heed to, cherish) the Lord. God wants us to acknowledge Him, have a relationship with Him, be betrothed to Him, and in Him alone find the deepest source of love. Oh … we get so distracted! But God's love is the key—the necessary component—to living a full life. It is the key of God's love that will enable us to live in love toward others.

• Do the following definitions of *acknowledge* represent your current relationship with God? Put a check mark beside those that do, and an X beside those that don't.
  ❏ *Recognize*—Do you recognize that God is your Maker and holds the blueprint for your life?
  ❏ *Be acquainted with*—Do you know Him in daily relationship?
  ❏ *Appreciate*—Do you have a habit of thankfulness for who He is and His faithfulness toward you?
  ❏ *Give heed to*—Do you read His Word and take His instruction seriously?
  ❏ *Cherish*—Do you hold close to your heart all that He is and the example He sets forth for living?

Each day is a precious gift. Each day also holds within it the ability to cause stress, anxiety, troubles, and disappointments. When these things play havoc with us, it's easy to see why we become locked up. It's as if we are bound from seeing the things of the Spirit because we are so focused on everything else around us. It is vitally important to have the right key. *Jesus* is the key that will unlock us from the distress and the loveless times we experience in the "real world."

Father,
I acknowledge You today. Forgive me for the times that I don't remember You—for the times I live in my own strength. I ask You to fill me with Your love. Come now and pour through my life and draw others to You through the power of Your love working in and through me. I realize that loving others might be a challenge, but I ask You to do the impossible inside of me. Amen.

DAY TWO: FINDING HOPE IN JESUS

1. Read Matthew 22:36–40.

Do you ever wish you could ask God to show you what the most important thing in life is? Well, that is what we find in this passage in Matthew. When asked what the greatest commandment is, Jesus responded with the two aspects of love—loving God with every part of us and loving others. It is clear that learning to walk in love toward others is something to make a priority in our lives. Jesus stated the most important commandment, and it's about relationship—not religion. He was speaking to the Pharisees, and they had religion and understood religious things, but what they needed was relationship. Remember, being a Christian is not about following rules; it's a matter of the heart.

• Write out Matthew 22:37.

The word *love* here in the original language is *agapao,* the verb tense of *agape,* which is God's unconditional love. In the Greek language *agape* represents something greater than what most of us can imagine, because *agape* is God and no one can fully understand or comprehend God. It is not the same as human love. C. S. Lewis distinguished between what he called "Need-love … which sends a lonely or frightened child to its mother's arms" and "Gift-love … which moves a man to work and save for the future well-being of his family which he will die without sharing or seeing."[2] Human love almost always has a Need element to it. But God's love is always Gift-love, with no strings attached and no selfish motives.

The apostle John tells us that love is at the core of who God is (1 John 4:8). Love is a Person. God's love is not based on
  • human understanding
  • human desires
  • human emotions

- others' responses
- our circumstances

Agape love is dependent on God—He never changes, neither does His love.

2. To define God's love, read how God Himself describes His love in 1 Corinthians 13:4–8.

- Read theses verses in several translations to get the full impact of the definition of God's love. What are some characteristics of this love that stand out to you as notable or unusual?

God's love is *not* human love. This is where we so often get confused. God's love is supernatural love. It's not dependent on human understanding, human desires, or human emotions. God's love is only dependent on God, who is always faithful and never changes. No matter how we feel or what we think, no matter how another person responds to us, and no matter what circumstance we are in—God always has love for the other person, even when we don't.

The true nature of God's love is not easily understood, and this is why the enemy of our souls has a heyday with us. It's important that we are educated and learn what God's love is so that we can learn to receive it, live in it, and give it out.

CHARACTERISTICS OF GOD'S LOVE

- Unconditional—He loves despite how the other person responds.
- One-sided—It doesn't have to be returned to be kept alive.
- Freeing—It's a love that not only lets us be who we really are but also frees the one we love to be himself or herself. All relationships are affected when we love like this.
- Other-centered—It's a giving love that puts another's interests above one's own.

3. Read John 15:4–7.

• Where must you remain if you are going to bring forth the fruit of God's love?

• What does this mean?

God wants to be as close to us as a branch is to a vine. One is an extension of the other. It's impossible to tell where one starts and the other ends. The branch isn't connected only at the moment of bearing fruit. The gardener doesn't keep the branches in a box and then, on the day he wants grapes, glue them to the vine. No, the branch constantly draws nutrition from the vine. Separation means certain death.[3]

—MAX LUCADO

• What are you like, when not living the connected life? (See John 15:6.)

Father,

I thank You for Your love. It's so beyond anything that I can fully understand, but I ask You to make it a reality in my life. I want to be mindful of how Your love is different than my human kind of love. I desire You, Your love, and Your life to be my daily relational reality. I am asking You to do what only You can do by pouring Your love into my very being. Amen.

DAY THREE: THE CONNECTED LIFE

Fruit is a by-product of the branch being connected to the vine. When the branch gets its nourishment from the vine, fruit grows naturally and freely. In the same way, God's love and the fruit of that love will naturally become evident in you as you live the connected life. Connected to Christ Himself. This kind of fruit doesn't just happen by our involvement in church, good works, good choices, or willpower. It is produced by a life connected to the Father. A life that is receiving power and love each day from the Source of all power and love.

1. Write out the different aspects of the fruit of God's Spirit as found in Galatians 5:22.

• Do you think these qualities would be helpful in personal relationships? Explain.

• How do you get this fruit?

2. Read John 17, the entire chapter.

As you read, keep in mind that this is Jesus praying for His disciples. He is praying for those who are His, so this applies to us as well. Pay close attention to what He is saying to the Father about you.

In John 17, I find hope in the following truths.
• He has authority over me (v. 2).
• He gives me eternal life (v. 3).

- I am His (v. 10).
- I am protected (v. 12).
- I am given joy (v. 13).
- I have His Word (v. 14).

• Write out John 17:15–17.

Sanctify means to set apart. Here Jesus is asking the Father to keep us set apart by the Word of God, which is the truth. He also tells us that the truth of His Word will set us free (John 8:32). We can see that it is the heart of Jesus and the plan of the Father that we would be *set apart and set free.*

I have made Your Name known to them and revealed Your character and Your very Self, and I will continue to make [You] known, that the love which You have bestowed upon Me may be in them [felt in their hearts] and that I [Myself] may be in them (John 17:26 AB).

Unlocked from the patterns of this world, we become free to love God's way. We become free to live in the will of our Father. We become free to have a relationship with God, the Maker of all things, including our hearts and the hearts of others.

3. Write out John 17:26.

• What does Jesus pray will be in you?

He Himself in me? Wow … now that is a powerful possibility! Even as I write this, I am getting ready for a meeting with a woman who is demanding, difficult, and rude. Her agenda for today is to chew me up! Could it be that God could express His very character to this woman through me today? Could He possibly give me the grace to be kind to someone who is mistreating me?

Once we recognize (get it firmly established in our minds) that God Himself lives in us and wants to work through us, life becomes different. It is this type of lifestyle that I liken to an "E" ticket ride. I know that I am dating myself, but when Disneyland first opened the Magic Kingdom there were ticket books for entrance to the rides. The tickets ranged in value from the A ticket to the E ticket. The E ticket was the best ride in the park, which at the time was the Matterhorn, while the A ticket at the time was the Great Moments with Mr. Lincoln theater.

Life can be an E ticket as we experience the exciting adventure of watching the power of a living God change us and work in and through us. Or, it can be an A ticket—a slow, just-trying-to-get-by lifestyle. God wants the best for His children, and the best is believing the truth and living in His power each day.

4. Read John 15:5–12.

• Take note of the following verses and write out how each one can apply to your personal life.
verse 5: If a woman remains in Christ and Christ remains in her, she will bear the fruit of love, joy, peace, etc.

verse 8: Bearing the fruit of Christ brings the Father glory.

verse 9: Remaining in the Father's love is staying connected in relationship with Him and obeying His Word.

verse 11: By remaining in the Father's love, our lives and our joy are complete.

• Write out John 15:12.

• How has the Father loved you?

• What are some characteristics of the Father's love toward you (1 Cor. 13; Gal. 5:22)?

5. Read John 15:13–17.

• How can you become God's friend?

• Write out John 15:16–17.

• What did God appoint you to do?

• What is His command, and how does this relate to your life and relationships today?

Father,

Show me how I become disconnected from You. Help me see things I do that cause me to live further away from You than is healthy for me. Change my heart. Give me the desire to remain in You each day and make necessary adjustments in my life—in order to remain in You. Amen.

DAY FOUR: THE CHOICE CHALLENGE

1. Read Joshua 24:14–24.

• According to this passage, what were the people of Israel committing themselves to do?

• What were two things that had to go, if they were to make this choice (v. 23)?
1.

2.

2. Read Deuteronomy 30:19–20.

• Write out Deuteronomy 30:19.

• What are you to choose?

• What will making this choice accomplish in your life?

Because God did not program us as robots, we have the possibility of choice. Loving others and choosing God's way will not be an easy adventure. It will be a challenge. Perhaps one of the most difficult challenges you have ever faced. You are probably thinking, *Wait a minute! I thought you said*

God's love was going to pour through me. How could that be a challenge? Well, the challenge comes in making the CHOICE to love. You must make a choice to follow God's way rather than submitting to your own selfish heart. The choice itself does not empower you, God's Spirit does the empowering. Your choice simply sets your heart in a given direction.

In Joshua 24:15, Joshua told the Israelites, "Choose for yourselves this day whom you will serve." Joshua knew there was a choice to be made—a directional choice. Once we say, "Lord, I choose You and Your way of loving others over my ways," God begins to work. But, it is a journey, a process, and a daily learning experience. There is no quick fix. Each day we have a choice! Choose this *day* whom you will serve. Will it be yourself, or will it be God? If you choose to serve yourself, then surely your love will be conditional at best. If you choose to serve God, then the power of God's Spirit will work in you, enabling you to love in an unconditional Christlike fashion.

The power comes from God, and the power of God is made available to us through relationship with Jesus Christ.

3. Read 1 John 3:11–24.

• What is the message that has been preached since the beginning (v. 11)?

• What have you passed from, and why (vv. 14–15)?

• What are you to choose this day (Deut. 30:19)?

• What is the pattern for relationships that Jesus left for you to follow (1 John 3:16)?

- How are you to love (1 John 3:17–18)?

4. The Target List

Now make a list of people to whom you are connected on a regular basis. These are the people whom God has placed in your life. Not one of these relationships is an accident. The list might include immediate family, other relatives, coworkers, neighbors, ex-spouse, in-laws, ex-laws, friends, children, and so on. Include all people—the good and the not-so-good relationships.

This is your target list. Your daily choices create a ripple effect—either good or bad—that touches all lives around you. Your goal with this list is to leave the mark of Jesus in your relationships with these people that God has placed in your life. Some people on this list are easy for you to love. You may have the same interests and similar personalities. Others are difficult if not downright impossible to love. But God promises to give us all that we need if we choose His way over ours.

Let's look at how the Bible addresses the impossible challenges, such as loving the unlovable.

> For it is God who works in you to will and to act according to his good purpose (Phil. 2:13).

5. Write out the following verses that address the word *impossible*.

Luke 1:37

Luke 18:27

Matthew 17:20

Hebrews 11:6

6. Now look up and write out the dictionary definition of the word *impossible*.

After writing out these scriptures, do you still think it is impossible to love some of those people on your list? What about when you are worn out and too tired to even crack a smile? Impossible? What about when someone has hurt you so deeply that you just want to run and hide? Impossible? Your problems are now God's possibilities! It is not impossible for us to love because we have the source of love living inside of us. But we must remember that it is God's love and not a counterfeit or fake love that we want to pour through us. It is a genuine work of the Spirit that we are trusting God for in our relationships. He is the Source.

7. Once again read 1 Corinthians 13—let's look again at love.

Many people refer to this Bible passage as the Love Chapter. We can see in this chapter the characteristics of God's love toward us, and we can also see God's pattern of loving others with that same love. For example: God is patient and kind with us, and it is His patience and kindness that can pour out through us to others as well. These attributes of God's love are the very traits that He can work into our hearts and lives as we abide in Him. His love is our pattern.

• Make a list of the qualities or characteristics of love—the patterns of Christ that you see in these verses.

• Which of these qualities also characterize you in your relationship with others? Place a check mark beside those. Place an arrow pointing to those qualities you don't see in the way you relate.

Father,

I commit to You all the people on my list. They are now the objects or "targets" of love. I am asking You to love these people through me. Teach me to walk in Your ways so that I will be a vessel ready for You to use to pour out love to others—especially these people You have placed in my life. Amen.

 DAY FIVE: RUNNING AFTER LOVE

1. Write out 2 Timothy 2:22.

• According to this verse, what are the four things you are to pursue?

1.

2.

3.

4.

• Look up the dictionary definition of *pursue* and write it here.

I like this definition of *pursue*: to chase or run after. This definition helps me to see clearly that a directional choice is the first step. If I am running after something, I am progressing in a given direction. I have a goal and I am going toward that goal. Today I want to make a choice to chase after love! I can see clearly that it is God's will for me to pursue, follow after, chase, and choose love.

In 1 John 4:16 we see that God is love. In 1 Corinthians 13 we find the characteristics of God's love. Living a life of love is a change in lifestyle. Living love is different from living in our own natural tendencies and our own behaviors toward people. We naturally love those who love us, but now God has a better way.

2. Read 1 John 4:7–12.

• What is the main theme of this passage?

• Where does love come from?

• What is made complete in you if you love others (v. 12)?

My beloved friends, let us continue to love each other since love comes from God. Everyone who loves is born of God and experiences a relationship with God. The person who refuses to love doesn't know the first thing about God, because God is love—so you can't know him if you don't love. This is how God showed his love for us: God sent his only Son into the world so we might live through him. This is the kind of love we are talking about—not that we once upon a time loved God, but that he loved us and sent his Son as a sacrifice to clear away our sins and the damage they've done to our relationship with God. My dear, dear friends, if God loved us like this, we certainly ought to love each other. No one has seen God, ever. But if we love one another, God dwells deeply within us, and his love becomes complete in us—perfect love!

—1 JOHN 4:7–12 MSG

3. Read 1 John 4:13–16.

• Have you acknowledged that Jesus is the Son of God? If so, how?

• Who lives in you at that point of acceptance and acknowledgment (v. 15)?

• On what then do you rely?

The focus here is on the fact that God loves us; therefore, we are to love others with the same love that has been freely given and poured into us. We don't deserve God's love. Many people you know don't deserve your love either—just thinking about their actions may make you cringe. Yet, just as we are not perfect, God calls us to a higher place of loving other imperfect ones. If we are to continue on in the Lord, we must daily choose to set our hearts toward a *lifestyle change* of love.

Living to love should be our life pursuit. This lifestyle of love should be our goal because Jesus Himself clearly outlined in the Gospels that it was His plan for us to be a loving people. This pursuit is clearly not based on making ourselves happy, but on making Jesus Master of our lives. In so doing we will also become happy women. Why? Because when we put God and His Word first, we are walking in the Spirit. The mind set on the Spirit is full of peace (Rom. 8:6). Jesus tells us in John 15:11 to remain in His love, then He lets us know why He has given this instruction: "so that my joy may be in you and that your joy may be complete." Do you want joy? Remain in His love!

The world we live in has purpose and joy all turned around. The focus is on being true to ourselves and pleasing ourselves. But all we get when we live to please ourselves is a selfish, self-absorbed heart. Living to please God and love others will take us out of the empty world of self and into new heights with our heavenly Father. In us is a place where we experience the fullness of joy as His joy, and our joy is complete.

Learning to love when it is not convenient is part of this lifestyle change. Just look at the words of Max Lucado as he illustrates this point in the following story.

> *My first pet came in the form of a childhood Christmas Eve gift. Somewhere I have a snapshot of a brown-and-white Chinese pug, small enough to fit in my father's hand, cute enough to steal my eight-year-old heart. We named her Liz.*
>
> *I carried her all day. Her floppy ears fascinated me, and her flat nose intrigued me. I even took her to bed. So what if she smelled like a dog? I thought the odor was cute. So what if she whined and whimpered? I thought the noise was cute.*
>
> *Mom and Dad made it clear in our prenuptial agreement that I was to be Liz's caretaker, and I was happy to oblige.... Within a few days, however, my feeling changed a bit. Liz was still my dog, and I was still her friend, but I grew weary with her barking and she seemed hungry an awful lot. More than once my folks had to remind me, "Take care of her. She is your dog."*
>
> *I didn't like hearing those words—your dog. I wouldn't have minded the phrase "your dog to play with" or "your dog when you want her" or even "your dog when she is behaving...." That's when it occurred to me, I am stuck with Liz. The courtship was over, the honeymoon had ended. We were mutually leashed. Liz went from an option to an obligation, from a pet to a chore, from someone to play with to someone to care for. Perhaps you can relate.... Only instead of being reminded, "She is your dog," you're told, "He is your husband" or, "He is your child, parent, employee, boss, or roommate."* [4]
>
> —MAX LUCADO

• Where will you turn when the honeymoon is over in your relationships?

• What happens when the person you once loved becomes a chore?

• What will be your choice today?

4. Write out Jude 20–21.

• In what are you to keep yourself?

We are instructed to *choose* this day what we will believe, whom we will serve, how we will live. This choice is a challenge. There came a time in my adult Christian life when I was faced with tough relationship choices. I had been hurt by a divorce, hurt by Christians, and hurt by the cold reality of a life that didn't turn out the way I had planned. I was mad at the world!

My inner turmoil led me to justify some very ugly actions that were certainly not appropriate for a Christian. I felt myself sink deeper and deeper into the pit of hate and despair. I was in agony. Then one day, a wise man gave me great advice. He looked me straight in the eyes and said, "I know you have been hurt, but your hurt will carry on in your children if you do not give it to God. Do you want your children to have a legacy of hate, hurt, and bitterness, or do you want to give them the legacy of love and forgiveness? You can't tell them about God's love if you aren't first walking in that love yourself."

I would like to say that I snapped out of my pain and from that day on I behaved perfectly! But ... you guessed it ... that was not the case. I did, however, make a choice that day—a choice to open up every part of me to God for healing and wholeness. It was then that I began learning how part of being completely whole is learning what it means to live in God's love. The choice was mine, the power to heal and deliver was God's. Jesus met me at the crossroads of love and hate. And, as a result of His power working in me, I have experienced God doing the impossible in my heart of hearts. I praise God for the legacy of His love.

Father,

Sometimes I think it would be easier if I were a preprogrammed robot. But, in reality I am thankful that You made Your people capable of making choices. I desire to choose life in Your Spirit. Walking in Your love toward others is choosing life. It is a serious endeavor. For when I do not choose love and the walk of love, I am in darkness. Impress on my heart how important it is to love as I am loved. And, as each new challenge emerges, speak gently to my heart: "Child, you have a choice." Father, now empower me to make choices that will please You, by the mighty power of Your Spirit, who works in me to will and to do of Your good pleasure. Amen.

Journal Page

- Are there any tough choices that come to mind in your life today? Explain.

KEY POINTS FROM LESSON 1

- Most of our lives we have learned to operate from human love.
- Human love is a feeling we live in. If we don't "feel" it, we don't love.
- Human love is selfish.
- Human love wants satisfaction in return, or love ceases.
- God has a better way to love—His love poured upon our hearts and into others.
- God's love is different from human love. *Agape* is the word for God's unconditional love. It is supernatural.
- God is love—love is a Person. We don't fully understand God, so we don't fully understand *agape* love.
- We were created for a love relationship with our Maker—created to love God and to love others.
- We must receive Christ in salvation in order to receive this supernatural love.
- Once we have received His love, we must stay connected to Christ to bear the fruit of love.
- We must acknowledge the Lord if we are going to grow up in Christ.
- We get to choose which way to set our hearts and which direction to live our lives.
- We can choose life in Christ or relational death by living only for self.
- God's love is the key that unlocks our lives.

Living Love ... As God Has Loved Us

LESSON 2

God's ultimate purpose is that His Son might be exhibited in me.
—OSWALD CHAMBERS

Since God so loved us, we also ought to love one another.
—1 JOHN 4:11

We all want to be treated fairly. When we are treated unfairly at the hands of another Christian, we are shocked and amazed. "This is not right," we say. "This is not how Christians should act!" Yet, the circle of unfairness goes round and round, as we too hurt others. We get sloppy with our words, we fail to protect those who belong to Christ, and we act in ways that are not pleasing to God. We are hurt when gossip is hurled at us, but we continue to talk about others, don't we? We are incensed when misunderstood but are quick to pass judgment ourselves. Cover it up all you want, but the truth is God sees it all!

Sometimes the way we treat others is just nonsense. Sadly, Christians are known to shoot their wounded. Christians can be rude, arrogant, exclusive, and unloving. Rather than being a vessel of peace and love, the church can often be a vessel of hurt and confusion. In a perfect world, we would all "get it" and understand the importance of loving one another. But we are not perfect—we are people, and people need the Lord.

God demonstrates His love to us every day. He loves imperfect ones like you and me. Now, let's pray for the power to give God's love to others in the same way God freely gives it to us.

DAY ONE: LIVING IN GOD'S DESIGN

1. Read 1 John 4:16–21.

• What is God (v. 16)?

• In this world, whom are you to be like (v. 17)?

• Why do you love (v. 19)?

• What are you if you love God and hate others (v. 20)?

• Write out 1 John 4:21.

Stumble: to lose one's footing, to make a false step, to lose balance.[1]

• Think of the "brothers" in your life—a spouse, child, parent, employee, boss, relative, or roommate. How does God want you to relate to these people?

2. Read 1 John 2:9–11, and rewrite this passage in your own words.

We are fooling ourselves if we talk the great talk of faith in God, and then turn with a knife in the back on those that God loves. Notice the word *stumble* here in this passage. When I walk in the light of God's love, there is nothing to make me stumble.

But, when I walk in hate and animosity toward another, I lose my balance in life. The word *hate* here comes from the Greek *miseo*, which means to detest, to persecute, to love less. The word *detest* can mean *dislike* and *feel hostility*. It is important to break down the meaning of this word, because I think we fool ourselves by thinking, *I don't hate anyone!*

> Jesus said, "Love the Lord your God with all your passion and prayer and intelligence." This is the most important, the first on any list. But there is a second to set alongside it: "Love others as well as you love yourself." These two commands are pegs; everything in God's Law and the Prophets hangs from them (Matt. 22:37–20 MSG).

However, the truth is that even when we refuse to give people a chance, disliking them and judging them, we begin acting in a false way. We smile and behave as if everything is fine, while secretly disliking them. Then we lose our footing because in such a place we are actually in darkness. Sometimes in this place our false sense of being okay has blinded us, and we don't realize how far we have come from fellowship with God. We may pride ourselves in not "hating" another, but according to the definition, if we love less than we are called to, we have an area and relationship to examine.

3. Write out Matthew 22:37–39.

Remember the word *love* here is *agapao,* which means to totally give ourselves over to something greater than ourselves. It's what we give our will and our life to. It's what we put first in our lives.

4. Write out Colossians 1:16.

• What are the key words?

No matter what your current personal circumstances are, God has created you for Himself and has called you for two basic purposes:

1. Love the Lord with every part of yourself.

2. Love others as you love yourself.

Are we to love ourselves? There is no scripture that says Jesus ever loved Himself. What happened was

- the Father loved (*agapao*) Jesus (John 15:9);
- Jesus accepted the love of the Father into His life;
- because He was an open and clean vessel, Jesus was able to pass that love of the Father on to us. This is our example.

As we love God, we can be a vessel to love others. We never focus on the need to love ourselves, because God has already given us all the love we need (1 John 3:16; John 15:19, 12; 17:26). We need to accept God's love into our lives; then we become a vessel of that love to pass on to others. Becoming lovers of self is not God's plan for us.

5. Look up the following verses and jot down the key truth of each one.

Revelation 12:11c

Luke 14:26

John 12:25

Acts 20:24

We are to *agapao* God and we are to *agapao* others. We accept God's love into our lives and live it out towards others. Accepting and understanding God's love for us is so very important! Scripture doesn't say we are to spend hours and hours seeking to love ourselves. That would be self-absorption, and that is clearly not God's plan. But, we are to know God's Word and seek to understand the truth it represents. We are continually to fill ourselves with His truth for us, to combat the lies of hell, the lies of our pasts, and the lies of the culture we live in. Stay in His Word. Pursue the truth of God's love. Then make it a pursuit of your life to extend that love to others. Remember all of this is made possible by God's Spirit at work in us.

Father,
I receive Your love. I am thankful for it. I desire to be changed by it. I desire to love others the way You love and accept me. Remove from me all forms of self-seeking and cleanse my selfish heart. Amen.

 DAY TWO: RELYING ON THE HOLY SPIRIT

1. Read John 14:15–18.
• What did Jesus say He would do for you (v. 16)?

• What is the name of the Holy Spirit (v. 17)?

• Where is He at this very moment?

In John 14, Jesus was making it clear that He would be crucified. His followers didn't know what they would do once He went away. He had helped them so much, done many miracles, and made such a difference. They didn't want Him to die, to go away … they were afraid. But in His loving way, Jesus told them not to be afraid (John 14:1). He told them to trust in God, and then He told them of the provision of God's Spirit.

> *The Holy Spirit is God Himself, a person with whom you can enjoy a personal relationship. He is not merely an impersonal force or power or essence within the universe, but He is rather a person who can speak to you and to whom you can speak. He is a person who can guide you, who can help you, who can strengthen you, who can teach you the truth of God.… When Jesus told His disciples, "I will pray the Father, and He will give you another Helper, that He may abide with you forever" (John 14:16), He was encouraging His men to prepare for a new way in which God would thereafter be relating to them.[2]*
>
> —CHUCK SMITH

God is calling us to live in a new way, and it will be accomplished by His Spirit.

2. Write out Romans 12:9–10.

• What are two stances that you are to take toward another person (v. 10)?

• Look up the following words in the dictionary and write down the definitions.

devoted

honor

The Bible doesn't instruct us just to love and honor those who are wonderful to us. In Romans 12, Paul tells us we are to bless those who curse us! Imagine someone telling you off, I mean really cursing at you, hurting you, and defaming your character. What does the Word of God tell you to do in such a situation? Bless 'em! Love 'em! Grace 'em! Yes, that's right ... we are to learn to walk in love, because that is what God's Word tells us to do and because it pleases our heavenly Father. This type of love-walk is accomplished by relationship with God and the empowering of the Holy Spirit. It's like picking up your rental car and finding out you have been upgraded. Instead of getting a small budget car (your human strength), you are given the keys to a spacious luxury car (the power of God's strength through His Spirit in you). Do you want to argue and insist on the budget car? Or will you get excited and hop in the upgrade and paint the town? In much the same way, God is giving us more than we could ever afford for ourselves. He gives us the power of His Spirit. Are we going to argue and insist on keeping our puny strength and worn-out effort, or are we going to take what He gives us?

3. Read Ephesians 4:1–6.

• Write out Ephesians 4:2.

• What are the key thoughts in this verse?

4. Read Ephesians 4:17–24.

• Write out Ephesians 4:23–24.

- According to these verses, what is to be made new?

- When embarking on any lifestyle change, what is the first thing to be changed?

- What is your part in a choice? (Refer to the "put on" part of the passage.)

- What is the new self supposed to look like?

Father,

I desire to live a life that matches the calling of being Yours. It is often confusing, because I want my own way and I get in the way of paying attention to Your example. Help me to care about Your example and not just blow it off. Impart wisdom to me that I might have a true lifestyle change in this area. Amen.

 DAY THREE: LIVING BY EXAMPLE

1. Read Ephesians 5:1–2.
- Who are you to imitate?

- How would this change your life and relationships with others?

We see the ideal and understand what God intended us to be, and in our heart we desire to live a life of love and purity, righteousness, truth, and peace. But then somehow we imagine we can achieve that goal by sheer effort and brute resolve. Yet the mere desire to be like Jesus doesn't itself create the reality. It doesn't enable us to realize our goal. We do not become like Christ by imitation, which is where a lot of people go awry. Jesus once said to Peter after he had failed yet again, "The spirit indeed is willing, but the flesh is weak" (Matt. 26:41 KJV).

> Therefore be imitators of God [copy Him and follow His example], as well-beloved children [imitate their father] (Eph. 5:1 AB).

> *I am certain that all of us have found this to be true in our own experience. We don't lack desire; it isn't that our spirit is unwilling. The problem is that our flesh is weak. That's why mere imitation will never work.... God wants to conform us to the image of His Son. That's the work He is doing in our lives through the Spirit.[3]*
>
> —CHUCK SMITH

2. Write out Romans 8:29.

• What work does God do in your life?

• How will this change you, making you more like Christ in love and life?

What a beautiful Helper the Holy Spirit is! And how we need His help to lead a successful Christian life. We need Him to indwell us, to lead us and empower us. We need His presence, we need His power, we need His leading. We need to walk in the Spirit so that we will not fulfill the lusts of our flesh. The flesh life is very strong; only God's Holy Spirit is stronger.[4]

—CHUCK SMITH

It is funny to me that even though we are Christians, we use the methods of the world and its psychology to determine how we will "really" live and how we will "really" find happiness. We have a preoccupation with ourselves, our feelings, and our rights. Many Christians are not convicted at all when they treat others poorly if they justify themselves. This is not God's way; it is the way of the world. In Ephesians 5 we can clearly see that we are to

- love;
- imitate God;
- put on the new self;
- find out what pleases the Lord.

Don't love the world's ways. Don't love the world's goods. Love of the world squeezes out love for the Father. Practically everything that goes on in the world—wanting your own way, wanting everything for yourself, wanting to appear important—has nothing to do with the Father. It just isolates you from him. The world and all its wanting, wanting, wanting is on the way out—but whoever does what God wants is set for eternity.

1 JOHN 2:15–17 MSG

3. Read 1 John 1:5–10.

- What does this passage say about sin?

- What is it saying regarding darkness and light in relationships?

• Do you have unloving areas in your life that you need to confess to God? What are they?

Lord,

Forgive me for all the times I have tried to love the world's way. I want to follow You, imitate You, and love Your way. Amen.

 Day Four: Taking Responsibility

1. Write out Psalm 139:23–24.

Psalm 139 gives us a map to starting each day. In this psalm we can embrace four core truths that cause us to respond to life differently. This different response also changes how we respond to others.

The four truths are

• He knows me (vv. 1–4);

• He protects me (vv. 5–12);

• He made me (vv. 13–16);

• He values me (vv. 17–18).

The response to God's love for us and His involvement in our lives is to take a stand on God's side—by loving what He loves and hating what He hates (Ps. 139:19–22).

The surrender to God's love is (Ps. 139:23–24)

• search me;

• cleanse me;

• fill me;

• use me.[5]

> If someone claims, "I know him well!" but doesn't keep his commandments, he's obviously a liar. His life doesn't match his words. But the one who keeps God's word is the person in whom we see God's mature love.... Anyone who claims to be intimate with God ought to live the same kind of life Jesus lived (1 John 2:4–5 MSG).

If you are going to embark on the path of living God's love, it's like Wheaties for the soul. When kids have extra energy, we sometimes say, "They ate their Wheaties this morning!" Well, when you are loving despite the circumstances, it's because you were with God eating those spiritual Wheaties of

- Adoration—I worship You today, God. I thank You for Your love.
- Confession—I need You today, Forgive me of my sins. Pour Your love into me for others.
- Thanksgiving—I thank You for every person and every thing in my life today. Make me an instrument of love, mercy, compassion, and blessing.
- Supplication—I pray for Your love in every relationship. Forgive me when I fail to see others through Your eyes, and give me a fresh surrender today to the process of being emptied before You in order to love others.

2. Read the following two passages.

- Psalm 133:1–3.

Look up the word unity *in a dictionary. What does it mean?*

Where does God bestow His blessings?

- John 17:10–11.

Who were people, even those you struggle with, been created by?

Who do you belong to?

What is Christ asking the Father here?

It is clear that God has called us to live in unity and to live a life of love. Throughout this study, keep in mind that our pattern of love is God Himself (1 Cor. 13). It would be helpful to read and reread 1 Corinthians 13 each week as you are renewing your mind in God's way of living out His love. Pray and ask the Holy Spirit to conform you to the image of Jesus, working into your life the pattern of God's love.

3. In the list of "love's obstacles" below, check the characteristics that generally apply to you in relationships.

LOVE'S OBSTACLES			
	defensiveness		*unforgiveness*
	anger		*bitterness*
	neediness		*hatred*
	stubbornness		*judgmental attitude*
	pain		*competitiveness*

Now pray about them in the way that David prayed in Psalm 139:23–24. Taking responsibility for wrong actions is an important part of Spirit-filled living.

4. In the following list of "love's pattern," check those things that you need more of in your life. Ask the Holy Spirit to work in you.

LOVE'S PATTERN			
	patience		*not self-seeking*
	kindness		*not easily angered*
	does not envy		*keeps no record of wrongs*
	not proud		*trusts/hopes*
	not rude		*perseveres*

Love is what we will show in our lives if we have got the love of God
shed abroad in our hearts. We will not have to go up and down the earth
proclaiming it. We will show it in everything we say or do.

—AUTHOR UNKNOWN

Father,

I desire to know what it means to love as You have loved me. I want to walk in love as You did. Not some flimsy, shallow love, but a real, abiding, authentic type of love. Oh, Jesus, I find this type of love so attractive, and my heart yearns to walk in a love that is not selfish and not looking for anything in return. Thank You for giving Yourself for me. Now may I learn to live to pour out and give myself for others. Fill me with Your love. Amen.

  DAY FIVE: UNBROKEN FELLOWSHIP

How good and pleasant it is when brothers live together in unity!

—PSALM 133:1

Fellowship simply refers to a friendly relationship or a union of peers. But, as we have discovered, fellowship is not always so simple. With the love of Christ, fellowship and love should be our goal. Even though we don't agree on everything and have different backgrounds, beliefs, and personalities, our goal should be friendly relations and courteous respect. Anyone can hate, complain, and hold bitterness. It takes a person believing in the power of a big and almighty God to go the extra mile and take the higher road. The extra mile is crucial to fellowship. The higher road is critical to the continued flow of the love of God.

1. Read Acts 2:42–47.

• To what did the early believers devote themselves?

- As a result of this devotion, what took place?

- How did they look after each other and the good of the whole body?

- What was the attitude of their hearts as they met together?

- What work of God happened daily as a result of their devotion to each other and to God?

- How can this apply to churches today?

2. Read 1 John 1:1–7.

In order to have fellowship with each other, we must first have fellowship with the Father. This is where some Christians fall into huge traps and wonder why their church relationships are sour.

- According to this passage, what will stop the flow of fellowship?

- What do you need to do to have proper fellowship?

• What does walking in the light mean in "real terms" to you today?

3. Read 1 John 2:7–11.

• What is the quickest way to go from walking in the light to walking around blinded in the darkness?

• What happens when you love your brother?

• Why are you more stable when you walk in love?

• When you choose the negative path of discord, what is the fruit of that choice?

4. Read 1 John 1:8–10.

• Where do you go when you know you have fallen short? Honestly.

• Do you think the pity party is the place to hang out? Why, or why not?

• If everyone sins, then why do you have such a hard time fessing up and getting on track again?

5. Write out 1 John 2:3–6.

This is powerful! We know that we are really connecting with the Father when we obey His Word. When we obey God's Word, love is made complete in us. Wow, I love that. Then comes the challenge.

• Write out 1 John 2:6.

WWJD? (What would Jesus do?) was a popular slogan a few years ago. It was on posters, bumper stickers, wristbands, and jewelry. It has a message. Are you picking up on the message beyond the catch phrase? We should always ask ourselves, "What would Jesus have me do in this circumstance, in this relationship, with my negative feelings, and so on?" Obviously, walking as Jesus did does not come naturally and does not come overnight. It also does not come without cost.

6. Read Matthew 16:24–25.

• What does following in Jesus' steps require?

Deny ourselves? Who are we kidding? We don't live in a society that accepts denial of our wants. We live in a society of quick fixes and instant gratification. The concept of self-denial is not widely embraced. But without it we will have a hard time living according to God's Word and living in fellowship.

Father,
Part of taking up my cross and giving You my life is denying myself. I admit that self-denial is not something I welcome or something I am used to. But in the area of relationships I must deny myself and live toward Your goal of love for me. Enable me to walk and live in this kind of self-sacrificing love. Amen.

Journal Page

- What one thing is God requiring of you as you do this study?

KEY POINTS FROM LESSON 2

- All things were created *by God and for God*—that includes us and the people in our lives.
- We are to love God with all of ourselves. This is commitment.
- God is Love. We are to know the truth of God's love and spend our days relying on it.
- We are not called to simply love ourselves, but to embrace and accept His love for us.
- There is no fear in love.
- Selfish actions come from control, and control is fear-based.
- There isn't a menu of options regarding whom we love.
- When living in our flesh toward others we become spiritually off-balance.
- God's wisdom always leads us down a path that causes deny of self.
- We are His, and we are to live to imitate Him.
- Taking responsibility for wrong actions or attitudes toward others is important.
- We are to be devoted to each other. This is another step in self-denial.
- WWJD? What would Jesus do with the people on your target list?

Living Love ... With a New Heart

LESSON 3

God has stood with His hands outstretched not only to take you but also for you to take Him. Just think of the invincible, unconquerable, and untiring patience of Jesus, who lovingly says, "Come to Me...."

—OSWALD CHAMBERS

The precepts of the LORD are right, giving joy to the heart.

—PSALM 19:8

It happened suddenly and without warning—at sixty-eight my mother's heart stopped as she suffered a massive heart attack. The family cried and prayed, and a determined young doctor tried everything. Once again her heart began to find a rhythm. Though she was immediately placed on life-support systems and suffered through a long recovery, she did live through that life-threatening attack. As she recovered in ICU, she was poked and prodded through test after test until the diagnosis was clear—the feeder system to her heart was destroyed. Then she was faced with a major dilemma: Would she be willing to undergo major heart surgery? It would not be a simple bypass, because every feeder vein in her heart was blocked, the main arteries as well as all the small ones. She was a time-bomb waiting to expire. Through the hands of a skilled doctor, she underwent major surgery and survived a twelve-way bypass—a rare surgery indeed. It gave her many more years of life. God was with her, He wasn't through with her yet ... and He healed her heart—literally! Once again the life flow of the blood was able to supply her body with all that it needed.

In much the same way, we too need a surgeon's touch on our hearts. I am not speaking of the heart muscle itself, but rather the heart of who we are. Jesus is the master surgeon who can unclog all of the arteries that lead to our heart of hearts. Our all-wise God can do spiritual surgery on the vessels that are clogged with things such as hurt, bitterness, misunderstanding, and unforgiveness.

Every person has a story. And usually that story has included some type of emotional hurt. Sometimes we get blocked or clogged in our personal pain. Even as Christian women, we are sometimes unwilling to yield certain parts of our hearts to God. We think He will make us love people we hate and like people we aren't interested in. Sometimes we just want to be left alone when it comes to relationships. But God has the way to health, and it is through living a life of love.

God has the power to heal our emotions and our hearts. As this tremendous healing takes place, we become free from fear, and we find ourselves becoming willing to love others with a new heart—the heart of Jesus.

This is a major breakthrough in our Christian lives. We need new hearts!

 DAY ONE: RECEIVING A NEW HEART

1. Read Ezekiel 11:14–21.

The book of Ezekiel is named after the prophet Ezekiel, whose name means "the strength of God." During his ministry Ezekiel proclaimed the basic message that Jerusalem and the people in it were doomed because of the sinfulness of their hearts and their idolatry. In this passage he gives those who are far away from the Lord new hope. The hope of a new heart. We know that Jesus came to give us a new life and is the fulfillment of a new heart and a new hope.

• In this passage, what does God promise to give us?

• What will be new?

Think of the difference between a heart of stone and a heart of flesh:
- heart of stone—dead, cold, hard, unable to feel
- heart of flesh—alive, warm, beating, keeping a proper rhythm

- Do you ever feel as if your heart is divided between what you feel like doing and what you know God wants you to do? Explain.

- As a Christian woman, what do the words *undivided heart* mean to you?

- Look up the dictionary definition for *divided*. What do you find?

- Write out Ezekiel 11:19, personalizing it by writing your name in place of the word *them*.

- Now journal what this verse is saying to you and how it could be applied to your life today.

A woman with an undivided heart is a woman with singleness of heart. She has one purpose: to live for God. But we all are human flesh with hearts that have become hard, deaf, and sometimes as immovable as a stone. God gives us hope that He can and will give us a heart transplant. He will give us a new, tender heart that is receptive and responsive to His Spirit. Do you need a heart transplant? What has happened to break your heart and challenge your hope?

2. Read Jeremiah 32:37–41.

God is gracious to the woman who repents, isn't He? Repenting is when we turn away from our wrongdoing, our wrong attitudes, and our sins. We come to God and ask Him to forgive us, and then we turn in the direction He is leading. This direction for most of us is a complete about-face! A 180-degree spin!

According to Jeremiah 32:39, why is it good to have a reverent fear of God?

For _____ and _____

• What does God "rejoice in doing" in your life (v. 41)?

Father,
You know the things that have hurt me. You are well aware of how hope has been snatched out from under me through the hurt I have experienced in relationships. I ask You to give me a new heart, a warm heart, a heart beating to Your rhythm. Amen.

   DAY TWO: WALKING IN HIS STEPS

1. Read Deuteronomy 5:29–32.
• What does verse 32 say you are to do?

2. Write out the following verses.
Deuteronomy 5:33

John 13:34

• According to these two verses, what are you to walk in?

3. Read Deuteronomy 6:1–5.

• What does verse 2 say will be affected if you obey and serve the Lord?

If we believe the children are the future, isn't it wise to raise them God's way? Too often we teach them a double standard. We talk about love, and we don't live in love. They aren't stupid. They read us like books, and unfortunately the book they often read in our actions is far from what they would find in the Bible.

Your children will follow your lead. If you are unkind, critical, and have a tendency to gossip, they will follow that pattern. As they get older, they will wonder how your Christian faith and your hard heart coexist! Isn't it time to get serious before God about our lives and our hearts?

4. Write out John 4:23–24.

• According to this passage, how are you to worship and live before God?

Believe me, woman, the time is coming when you Samaritans will worship the Father neither here at this mountain nor there in Jerusalem. You worship guessing in the dark;

we Jews worship in the clear light of day. God's way of salvation is made available through the Jews. But the time is coming—it has, in fact, come—when what you're called will not matter and where you go to worship will not matter. It's who you are and the way you live that count before God. Your worship must engage your spirit in the pursuit of truth. That's the kind of people the Father is out looking for: those who are simply and honestly themselves before him in their worship. God is sheer being itself—Spirit. Those who worship him must do it out of their very being, their spirits, their true selves, in adoration.

—JOHN 4:21–24 MSG

Do you ever fall into the trap of living by appearances only? People see the heart we have painted on us. They don't see the real heart, but God does. We can fool people with a nice smile and a timely word, but God is not interested in what we put on for others to see—God is interested in us living in spirit and in truth. He desires to give us a new heart so that we can live for Him in authentic relationships, worshipping in spirit and in truth by our genuine care for others. In so doing, we will be affecting lives all around us.

Father,
Make me a woman who lives a life of worship. A life that is authentic, honest, and up close and personal with You. Amen.

 DAY THREE: IMPRINTED WITH TRUTH

1. Read Deuteronomy 6:4–9.
• Write out Deuteronomy 6:5.

You can't give something that you don't have yourself. You can mentally acknowledge God's love, but it can still not be a heart reality. It's like being a thirsty person with a cup of water in front of you—yet never taking a drink.

- Review verses on receiving God's love:
  - Romans 5:8—We are loved.
  - Ephesians 1:5—It pleases God.
  - 1 John 4:8—It is His nature.
  - Romans 5:20—He is greater than our sin.
  - Ephesians 3:17–19—Pray to know the love of God.
  - 1 John 4:10–11—Give the love away to others.

2. Read Matthew 22:34–40. (Repetition of foundational directives is important to building a new core belief system.)

- According to Scripture, what is the most important thing in life?

- What is the second most important thing?

3. Write out Deuteronomy 6:7.

- What are you to impress on your children?

- How do you think that is accomplished?

• Do your children see the real you behind closed doors? What do they see?

• Could you use a new heart and a right spirit? Why?

It's the little things we do that mean a lot. But, often, the small things are viewed as insignificant. In reality the small things are important and are like the spices of life. We make a mistake if we are only interested in the main course, or the big things, because the main course without the spice of love is bland and tasteless. Remember that love is the salt of life.

4. Write out Matthew 5:13.

Lord,
Help me not to overlook the small things that I can do each day to add the spice of Your love to my relationships. Amen.

 DAY FOUR: LOVING AS A FAITH CHOICE

1. Read 2 Corinthians 5:7–10.

• How do these verses tell you to live?

• What should be your main goal in life?

- Does living in God's love please Him? How?

- For whom are we to live?

Ouch! So much of the time I just live for me. I attend my own pity parties, hardening my heart with mountains that I have made out of molehills! Can you relate? Do you know who originated the pity party? Well, I believe it was Satan himself. He thrives on the self-focus that is present when a woman begins to feel sorry for herself. He entices us with lies laced with truth bites. We take the bait and end up completely undone. We need to realize that he is the host of such a party, and he caters the party with the poison of lies. Get out and get out fast!

As Christ's love compels me, influencing me in the right direction, I become more and more convinced that the right way to live is *for Him*. This is huge when applied to all interpersonal relationships. Now I can let go of the small stuff that normally would send me over the edge. I become healed in my heart, and this affects my personality and my actions toward others.

2. Read 2 Corinthians 5:16–21.
- How are you to stop looking at people? What does this mean?

- What ministry did God give to you?

- What message has been committed to you?

• In verse 20 of this passage, what are you called?

We are representing Christ in this world—that is what the Christian life is about. But because we think it is all about "us," we get off track. Let's look at this idea of representation or being ambassadors of Christ. We are to represent God, and God is love—this is the nature of who God is. Jesus Christ His Son was sent to the world in God's love so that no one would perish. The very essence of Jesus Christ is love.

The message of reconciliation is the message of God's love for His people. His appeal is that of love. What are we doing then … living for ourselves, with hearts that are hardened to the people around us? We can sing a song, speak a praise, lift our hands, but are we God's ambassadors of love?

The most natural way to see someone is from a worldly point of view. What we see is that we get, mixed with our perceptions of who someone is. We see here in 2 Corinthians that we are no longer to look just at what we see, but instead to look at people as those Christ loves. In order to do this we need a new heart.

Father,
Forgive me for taking the bait too many times and wasting countless hours feeling sorry for myself over some perceived rejection or offense. I see who is enticing me to sit in my own stuff, and I want nothing to do with it anymore. I realize that if I make my problems precious, they will turn and poison me. Help me to stand. Amen.

 DAY FIVE: REBUILT AND RENEWED

1. Read Isaiah 61:1–7.

These verses speak of a people who are transformed by Jesus Christ. People formerly devastated, living in the midst of ancient ruins, now being restored, rebuilt, and renewed. Maybe you are living in the rubble of ancient ruins too. Your heart may need to be rebuilt and renewed. God, through Jesus, makes beautiful things of our hearts and lives as we submit ourselves to Him. Just look at some of the things He does for you, according to Isaiah 61:1–7.

- He preaches good news to your poor tired heart.
- He binds up the broken places in your heart.
- He proclaims that you can be free from the captivity of the negative impact of relationships.
- He releases you from darkness and from your prison of hate—through His Word.
- He comforts you as you cry and process some of the pain of life.
- He crowns you with beauty as He takes you out of the ashes.
- He anoints you with joy and gladness as He lifts you from your mourning.
- He wraps you in a new garment of praise, instead of your rags of despair.
- He calls you an oak of righteousness and displays splendor through you.
- He declares that you are His planting, so you can have confidence and bloom in His love.
- He rebuilds, restores, and renews you! Everlasting joy will be yours!

Wow! How wonderful that God provides all we need to live with new hearts.

As we continue to study, we will look at some areas that can clog the arteries if we are not careful to walk in His ways.

Let's stop right now and thank God for who He is and for the new heart He desires to give us. Today put on your Jesus glasses, and begin looking at life and love through a new lens. Take a good look at those you come in contact with, looking at them through your Jesus glasses, your new eyes of love. You will be surprised how refreshing it is to see people with God's eyes, viewing them from His viewpoint and loving them because they are His.

You are God's representative. In order to represent Him, you must know Him. In the business world, a sales representative knows the product and knows the manufacturer's goals and targets in marketing or representing it to the public. In the same way, we are to know Him and acquaint ourselves with His goals. We then move and live in those goals, because we are representing Him. His goal is love, and in Isaiah 61 we can see how that love is played out in practical ways in our lives. Let's go forward with new hearts, tender hearts, willing hearts, yielded hearts—to love Him and love others.

2. Read 1 John 3:17–18. Jot down the key point.

Many people love things and use people to get their needs met. God intends for us to love people and use things to bless them. You must start where you are. One of the greatest joys in life is living to be a blessing to another.

3. Look up the following verses and write down what they say about how to love.
Proverbs 3:28

2 Corinthians 9:9

1 Timothy 6:7

1 John 2:15

4. Start a Blessing Box.

Get a box and begin collecting things around your house that someone else may need more than you do. Learn to be a radical giver. Some women have taken this idea and planned giving potlucks, where the hostess sets up a few tables and women can bring the things that they want to bless others with. Women come and take what they need, from purses, to clothes, to children's items, to books—the sky is the limit. Get creative with your giving and your love expressed through thinking of others first.

This is a fun activity for a women's group, moms' group, or church group to do too. Decorate a hall for a women's tea, breakfast, or dinner. Have tables set out for women to display their blessings to be given to others. After a meal and a short program on blessing others, let women shop the tables for things that they might be able to use. All things remaining can be donated to a women's shelter.

Father,

I need Your heart! So many things have hurt me, and so much junk is piled high in my heart that I am surprised it can even keep beating. I ask You to replace all hardness in my heart in relation to Your will or Your Word. Replace it with a willingness to love others and to serve You. Replace it with Your warm, caring, honest heart. I love You, Lord, and it is my desire to be called a minister of God as I represent You in my little corner of the world. Be glorified in me! Amen.

Journal Page

- What is the Lord calling you to give?

_____

_____

_____

_____

_____

_____

_____

_____

_____

_____

_____

_____

_____

_____

_____

_____

_____

_____

_____

_____

_____

KEY POINTS FROM LESSON 3

- God wants to give us a new heart.
- Some of us are living with a dead cold heart.
- God has the power to give us a new heart and a new spirit.
- Jesus came to create new life and new love in us.
- We are called to study His steps in relationships and walk in them.
- The time has come for God's people to be authentic in worship and love.
- I cannot give out anything I don't have myself.
- Be first a partaker of God's love.
- Impart the message of God's love to your children and family.
- Love is God's nature and His every move made on our behalf.
- Loving is a faith choice.
- Feeling sorry for myself is a trap from the enemy of my soul.
- I have everything to be thankful for—God's love completes me.
- I can live rebuilt and renewed in my relationships as I deny myself and live God's way.
- I am to live my life giving and blessing others.

Living Love ... Despite Our Hurts

I have to make an effort to keep my conscience so sensitive that I can live without any offense toward anyone. I should be living in such perfect harmony with God's Son that the spirit of my mind is being renewed through every circumstance of life.

—OSWALD CHAMBERS

Love is the soy sauce on the chop suey of life.

Hurt is a fact of life. You don't have to be a genius to figure that out. In fact, you don't have to go far to find hurting, needy people. Usually that person is as close as your own mirror. Who is she? Where has she been? How have life's hurts affected the image looking back at her? We can put on a smile, cover up the redness of eyes spent with tears, but within our hearts we know far too well that the hurts that have come our way have changed us. For some, the changes have been for the better. For others, the change has produced a bitter and defensive woman who is hard on the inside despite her outward loveliness.

Hurts come in many shapes and sizes. Hurts can harm us or help us. What will your choice be? Your personal hurt can be the stepping-stone to becoming a more mature woman, or it can be the tombstone that kills you with anger and bitterness. You can get bitter, or you can get better. The choice is always yours. God is there waiting to meet you at the crossroads of choice.

The dictionary definition of hurt is to experience pain, either physical or emotional distress; to cause harm, to damage, offend, to cause mental suffering.

Remember the verses in Hosea from lesson 1 about acknowledging the Lord? When we are hurt, it is especially important to acknowledge the Lord.

- to admit the reality of the hurt to the Lord
- to accept the truth of God's Word and acknowledge it before the Lord
- to express gratitude for God's presence with you, even in your pain

In order to deal with the hurts of real life we are dependent on God's *agape* love. Without it we are just living nice and putting a Band-Aid on our wounds. To *agapao* means to *lose self*. I realize this is not a popular statement. How about if I say to walk in *agape* we must get over ourselves! We

- choose to obey God's will and not our own desires;
- deny ourselves, our thoughts, emotions, and desires that are contrary to God's will;
- take a look at the hidden inner struggles that are often hard to give up;
- don't push down our feelings but bring them to the light of God's Word.

 DAY ONE: THE WARFARE OF LOVE

1. Write out 1 Peter 4:8.

- What is this verse speaking to you regarding a difficult relationship in your life?

We often think of spiritual warfare as being on our knees praying or confessing God's Word. Both have a place in the spiritual warfare of the believer. But did you ever stop to think that loving other people is actually spiritual warfare? First Peter 4:8 teaches us to have intense love for one another. In the King James Version the word is *fervent*. The verb form of the Greek word here means to be hot, to boil. Our love walk needs to be hot, on fire, boiling over rather than cold and barely noticeable.

Have you ever cooked something so long that it became too hot to handle? Well, that is the way

I want to be. I want Satan to dread my getting up each day because he knows I am committed to love—which is the way of the Father.

2. Read 2 Corinthians 10:3–5. Look up each of these key words in a dictionary or concordance, and write down what the word means.

weapons

divine

power

demolish

arguments

pretensions

We are in a war. Here we see that our weapons are not carnal, man-made weapons, but rather weapons that are mighty. The stronghold of cold love must be dealt with in our lives—cold love toward God and cold love toward people.

I believe that Satan has a high-tech spiritual warfare against the church, and he is using widespread selfishness as the bait. We have become so tuned in to our feelings that our feelings have become the barometer for our actions—rather than God's Word being the guiding factor. Purposely forgetting about ourselves and our problems and doing something for another person while we are hurting is one of the most powerful ways to overcome evil with good.

3. Write out Romans 12:21.

4. Read Luke 23:32–43. What was Christ's attitude toward those who hurt Him?

5. Read Acts 7:59–60. What was Stephen's prayer regarding those hurting him?

In each case we see that evil is overcome by counteracting it with good. When Jesus was on the cross He took time to comfort the thief next to Him, and when Stephen was being stoned, he prayed for those stoning him. How did you react the last time you were being treated unfairly? If we wage war against selfishness and walk in love, the world will take notice. Don't let selfishness win the war that is in front of you!

"But it's not my fault"—I say it myself, and I hear it all the time. Women ask, "Why should I be the one to give in?" The key here is taking responsibility for being the first to overcome the issue, the fault, the offense, with good. And in doing so, you will be walking in the light according to the directives in God's Word.

I can recall a time when I was unfairly treated. The other person was being stubborn and insensitive. I wanted to withdraw, which I did for a few days, but in the end I was miserable. Why? Because I was allowing my own pride and selfishness over hurt feelings to win the war. In the end I had no control over how the person felt about me, what she said about me, or how she treated me. Her actions were between her and God.

Things did not get resolved, because she didn't want to bend or budge. This was frustrating! But I had to do my part. I had to get over myself and submit the situation to God, and in the end the truth stood: I am called to overcome evil—hardship, misunderstanding, offense—with good. God was calling me to be courteous and kind, and to overlook the offense. Our friendship was never restored, but I know that obeying God's Word was a huge stepping-stone for me in the midst of a real-life relational crisis. I wanted to scream, to run, to hide—to do anything other than be the first one to make a kind move. Believe me when I say my pride was waging a war so huge that giving in to the Lord rather than myself was a turning point. I learned that this is the best way to live. Just recalling this instance puts a smile on my face, because I learned a tremendous life lesson in dealing with undesirable situations: God's way works!

6. Read Psalm 15. According to this psalm, the one who is blameless and does what is righteous also does what else? (Look for nine things.)

Righteous people keep their oaths even when it hurts. Wow! This is contrary to the world's way of handling things. The last verse of Psalm 15 makes it clear that we will not be shaken when we keep on trusting, but rather we will walk uprightly even when it hurts. Keep your commitment to God, and your commitment to living in love, even when it hurts.

> *There is only one being who loves perfectly, and that is God, yet the New Testament distinctly*
> *states that we are to love as God does; so the first step is obvious. If ever we are going to*
> *have perfect love in our hearts we must have the very nature of God in us. In Romans 5:5*
> *the Apostle Paul tells us how this is possible; he says "the love of God is shed abroad in our*
> *hearts by the Holy Ghost which is given unto us." He is speaking not of the power to love*
> *God, but the very love of God itself which is "shed abroad"—a superabounding word, it*
> *means that the love of God takes possession of every crook and cranny of our nature.*[1]
>
> —OSWALD CHAMBERS

Lord,
This is where the rubber meets the road. When I hurt I want to hurt others back. Help me to choose the higher way and win in the warfare of love. Amen.

DAY TWO: THE RESTORATION OF LOVE

1. Write out Psalm 71:20–21.

• What can God do even after you have been hurt or grown bitter?

• Write out the dictionary definition of *restore*.

I like the synonyms of *restore*—renew and revive. God has the power to renew and revive you even though someone has hurt you. First, we must follow the scriptural example and start by giving the burden of the hurt to God.

Humble yourselves, therefore, under God's mighty hand, that he may lift you up in due time. Cast all your anxiety on him because he cares for you (I Peter 5:6–7).

2. Read Psalm 55:22. What is the key point of this verse?

• What is the definition of *cast?*

3. Read Psalm 60:11. What does the psalmist tell us about God and about people?

4. Read Psalm 61:2. What key point is the psalmist making?

5. Read Psalm 62:8. What does this psalmist tell us that will help us love others?

6. Read Psalm 68:19–20. What does this psalmist say about God?

7. Write out Psalm 25:21.

David had enemies on every side. Yet, through it all he learned to lean on God and trust in God's unfailing love. Do you generally look to God through your hurts, or do you try to handle the situation on your own? I would say that probably most women try to fix things before giving them to God or following in His way.

• Honestly … how do you usually respond when someone hurts you? Mark the characteristics that apply to your response.

	get angry		give silent treatment
	fume		fight back inside
	become defensive		think of ways to get even
	plot to make offender see error		throw Scripture at offender
	gossip about offender		sulk
	turn others against offender		seek revenge
	act kindly despite offender's problem		trust God to handle offender
	pray for God to bless offender		eat
	cry		turn the other cheek

Lord,

Help me to identify the childish things I do in relationship with others. May my heart be open to change and to living in Your truth and freedom. Amen.

D{4}L   DAY THREE: THE RELATIONSHIPS OF LOVE

1. Read Ephesians 4:1–3.

• What is Paul urging you to do here?

Live _____

Be _____

Be _____

Make _____

2. Read Philippians 2:3–8. Do you usually look after only your own interests in an argument, or do you have the other person's heart and life in mind too? Explain.

Our selfishness and shortsightedness will cause us to act in *opposition* to the flow of God's Spirit if we do not watch out. Keep yourself on a short leash, so to speak, when it comes to your dealings with others who have hurt you. Do not defend yourself; do not be proud and vain. Ask God to empower you to quit thinking life is only about *you* and what "that person did to *me*." If we are to be lifted to new heights in our walk with God, we must learn to follow in His ways, even when doing so is hard, uncomfortable, or unnatural. Sometimes I feel as if God is saying, "Debbie, get over yourself!"

> We are to do nothing out of selfish ambition or vain conceit.

3. Write out Romans 12:14.

• What are you to do to people who hurt you?

• What are you not to do?

BLESS	CURSE
to honor	*to cause harm*
to pray for	*to cause evil to befall upon*
to ask for divine favor for	*to swear at in profane terms*
to confer well-being or prosperity upon	*to wish ill will and bad luck upon*

To love people we don't like is one of life's great challenges. It takes extra motivation and help from outside ourselves. For me, the greatest motivation to love people I don't like is God's love for me. When we struggle in our response to another person, we must remember that we are all sinners whom God has forgiven for many things. If we cannot forgive others for their sins against us, then perhaps we have lost sight of just how much we have been forgiven.[2]

—FLOYD McCLUNG Jr.

4. Read Romans 12:17–21.

• Write out Romans 12:18.

• Is it possible to do this? Why, or why not?

• What depends on me?

We need to get this ingrained in our minds. Payback is not God's will for His people. Prayer, not payback, is the way to win the war in hurtful relationships. This is such an important truth and guideline. It is easier to just lash out or resort to our unhealthy forms of communication and problem solving when someone hits us where it hurts. But we must *not!* Payback is not God's way.

Are you feuding with a friend, family member, coworker, or ex-spouse? Do not pay back the hurt this person caused you; it will only end up destroying you, and it is contrary to the way God would have you spend your time and energy. Remember, the way God desires us to spend our time and energy is in learning how to love Him with all of our being, and then to love others.

• Do you think peace is always possible? Explain.

5. Write out the following verses as an answer to the question, "How do we love Him?"
1 John 5:3

2 John 6

Galatians 5:14

Romans 13:10

Father,
In myself I want to stay mad, take revenge, or repay evil. It seems fair. But living fair is different than living in Your love. Teach me Your way. Show me the magnificent possibility of Your love flowing through me. Amen.

DAY FOUR: THE RESPONSIBILITY OF LOVE

In order to live differently we will have to unpack some of the baggage that we have been lugging behind us for years. Here are some of the things that will no longer work for us and just have to go. We must unpack the old and embrace the new.

Unpack selfishness. ➤➤ *Embrace laying down your will.*

Unpack old self and its attitudes. ➤➤ *Embrace the Spirit's life within you.*

Unpack imitation. ➤➤ *Embrace genuine faith in what is possible in Christ.*

Unpack human reasoning. ➤➤ *Embrace the truth according to Scripture.*

(Why should I be the one to change?) ➤➤ *(Because your spiritual life depends on it.)*

1. Write out Romans 12:16.

• What does this verse tell you to do in your relationships?

2. Write out Romans 12:19–20.

In this day of lawsuits and legal rights, Paul's words seem impossible and impractical. When someone hurts you deeply, instead of giving him or her what he or she deserves, give kindness. What does it mean to heap burning coals on someone's head? This may refer to an Egyptian tradition of carrying a pan of burning charcoal on one's head as a public act of repentance. By referring to this proverb Paul was saying that we should treat our enemies with kindness so that they will turn from their sins.

Obviously, it is not always possible for things to go smoothly in relationships. You, however, are only responsible for *your part* of the relationship; the Bible says "as far as it depends on you, live at peace with everyone" (Rom. 12:18). Many times I am the one who keeps the fire of hassle burning. I run swiftly to old methods of handling hurts. Sometimes I sulk, and other times I storm. And usually it is all because of my own pride! Sometimes it is because the hurt brings out an old insecurity that needs to be healed and made secure and whole by God's touch.

Don't waste time concentrating on blaming others. Sure, maybe they did something awful, but now what are you going to do with their awful behavior? Could it be happening so that you can understand yourself better, seek God more, and learn to love more fully?

3. Look back again at Romans 12:16.

This verse tells you two things you are not to be:
Do not be _____, and
do not be _____.

> Selfish: concerned only or primarily with oneself or one's own interest, not much regard for others, self-seeking, self-centered.

Sounds familiar, like the "selfish ambition and vain conceit" we looked at earlier. Selfishness causes many problems in our relationships. Selfishness causes us to hold on to hurts and offenses so tightly that our white-knuckled grasp can hardly be broken.

I cannot live in harmony if I am full of myself—full of pride. In this position I end up thinking everything needs to go my way or revolve around me. When I think too highly of myself, I am not humble before my heavenly Father, and I cannot hear the voice of God or the Spirit's direction in the middle of the hurt. Laying my life before the Father is necessary if I am going to learn to love despite the hurts that are hurled at me.

Selfishness is obviously contrary to God's ways. Love is not self-seeking and is not proud. Love also holds others in honor and high regard because it rejoices in the truth, protects, and hopes for the best in another's life.

4. Write out Romans 12:15.

Revenge: to impose or inflict injury in turn for injury.

Lord,
I so often act out of selfishness. I need to learn a new way of relating to others—based on Your example. I am a redeemed woman in a fallen world—give me the grace to live for You. In Your name, Amen.

D{4}L   DAY FIVE: STEPPING IN A NEW DIRECTION

1. Read Romans 12:20. How are you to treat an enemy or someone who has hurt you?

2. Write out Romans 12:21. Memorize this verse. (This is good 3 x 5 card material!)

• How do you suppose you can overcome evil with good? What are some practical ways that you can turn the other cheek or overcome the evil in a situation?

3. Read James 5:13-18.

This passage speaks of what to do when the rubber meets the road, or when your relationships hit the wall! There are many different ways we can deal with hurts. The choice we make in dealing with our hurts will affect the outcome. If we want to overcome evil, then we must *carefully* choose our way of handling people and situations. There is a saying, "Life is precious, handle with prayer." Well, life and people are both precious. We should pray until something happens! Elijah prayed earnestly, and what happened (vv. 17–18)?

> When they hurled their insults at him, he did not retaliate; when he suffered, he made no threats. Instead, he entrusted himself to him who judges justly (I Peter 2:23).

In every situation we have the following options:

1. Internalize and become bitter.
2. Pay back and try to get even.
3. Forgive and hand things over to Jesus.

INTERNALIZE

This is a game of pretend and pretense. When we grit our teeth, suck it all up, paste a happy smile on our face, we are only allowing the problem to go unresolved, making room for resentment and bitterness to grow. This way of handling an offense only allows us to become a pressure cooker ready to blow at the next slightest offense. Often we feel as if God isn't concerned with our little hurts so we try to hang on for dear life with our own strength. This does not work. We must cast our cares, hurts, worries, and fears on God because He cares for us (1 Peter 5:7).

> They called him every name in the book and he said nothing back. He suffered in silence, content to let God set things right (I Peter 2:23 MSG).

If you choose—*and, yes, it is a choice*—to internalize your hurts, holding tightly to them, you are allowing those hurts to sour your personality and all that God has created you to be. How can you have a countenance of joy and faith when you are harboring resentment and simmering in a pot of bitterness? You may also end up battling the hurdle of depression because depression is anger turned inward.

PAY BACK

We all know how to do this. I don't care if you are the most "spiritual" woman in the church; given the right fuel for the fire you know exactly how to pay others back for the hurt they have caused you. Remember, we are all imperfect flesh, and when we walk in the flesh, we will fulfill its lusts and passions. Paying back is walking in the flesh and not in the Spirit.

For it is commendable if a man bears up under the pain of unjust suffering because he is conscious of God (1 Peter 2:19).

Sometimes we silently pay back by holding a grudge against others. We foolishly think that our grudge will hurt them. What's really happening is that the offender is living "rent free" in our minds and harassing our every waking thought! Our offenders couldn't care less what we think, so our payback will not impress or affect them.

God's way is to love them, do good to them. Give a soft and gentle answer to their anger, and the Bible says that will turn away wrath (Prov. 15:1). You will probably not get instant results, but as you persevere, you will see God's faithfulness. Now, isn't that better than payback?

FORGIVE

Forgiveness is key in a Christian walk. Forgiveness is not forgetting that the offense happened, but it is giving it up and letting it go. This is much easier said than done, but we can do all things through Christ who has given us the strength to obey His Word and follow in His way (Phil. 4:13).

You may never get an apology from people who have hurt you. That's okay. Despite others' actions, you can be freed by examining your own actions. You can be freed by examining your own heart, owning your own feelings of hurt and anger, and asking God to work in the very heart of you and give you the ability and will to let go and trust Him.

Do you really want others' offenses to rule your life? You can wait for the apology that may

Do not conform any longer to the pattern of this world, but be transformed by the renewing of your mind (Rom. 12:2).

never come or you can ask God to show you His way of walking in love with people. Forgiveness is one of the keys that unlocks us and keeps our hurts from destroying our personality, health, and other relationships. Forgiveness is the antidote for the poison that begins brewing when we are wronged. Forgiveness is possible when you process through the pain of your hurt in light of God's Word, committing yourself and your feelings to God. You then move into a choice that makes His Word and His will the focus of your healing.

The key behind forgiveness is being conscious of God and being content to let God set things right.

The moment we start hating others, we become their slaves. When we obsess over wrongs done to us, we become more conscious of the wrongs that have come our way than the good that God brings into our lives. In this place we can't enjoy life the way we previously did, and we are plagued with angry thoughts, sour rumblings of the mind, and often physical symptoms. We may have trouble sleeping or eating. Some of us may fall into depression or sleep or eat too much! All the while those who hurt us are living their lives and doing their own thing. Doesn't it make more sense to submit to God and follow in God's way of love?

Doing things God's way will require a lifestyle change because it does not come naturally to our flesh nature. A lifestyle change happens when your mind is renewed (Rom. 12:2).

This verse means that when we put new ideas and truth into our minds over and over, our lives will begin to take on a new belief system, and our actions will follow our beliefs and new values.

From the time we were children, we learned to act in self-defense. As we grew to be adults, we were taught that it is important to stand up and be counted and defend ourselves. We are now told even as Christians that we must watch out for ourselves because nobody else will. Tell me, where is this principle found in Scripture?

Of course someone will watch out for me! My heavenly Father already knows what I need. He sees every offense; He knows my frame and the frame of my offenders. He can do incredibly more for me than I can do by watching out for myself, because He is a big and mighty and powerful God!

> You who are servants, be good servants to your masters—not just to good masters, but also to bad ones. What counts is that you put up with it for God's sake when you're treated badly for no good reason.... This is the kind of life you've been invited into, the kind of life Christ lived. He suffered everything that came his way so you would know that it could be done, and also know how to do it, step-by-step (1 Peter 2:18, 21 MSG).

In the Company of Roses

Roses are grown for the Vienna market in great profusion and with much distillation of fragrance.
We are told that if you were to visit that valley at the time of the rose crop, wherever you would
go the rest of the day, the fragrance you would carry with you would betray where you had been.
There is a beautiful parable given to us by the Persian poet Saadi. The poet was given a bit of
ordinary clay. The clay was so redolent with sweet perfume that its fragrance filled all the room.
"What are you, mush or ambergris?" he questioned.
"I am neither," it answered. "I am just a bit of common clay."
"From where then do you have this rare perfume?" the poet asked.
"I have companied all the summer with a rose," it replied.
We are just bits of the common clay of humanity. But if we company with the One
who is the Rose of Sharon … something of the fragrance of His life will pass into ours.
Then we will be a freshening and a sweetening influence to the world around us.[3]

—HENRY GARIEPY

Your hurts can make you a *better* woman or a *bitter* woman. With whom will you keep company when in the middle of life's hurts? Will you choose the sweet fragrance of Jesus today?

I have set before you life and death, blessings and curses. Now choose life, so that you and your children may live and that you may love the LORD your God, listen to his voice, and hold fast to him. For the LORD is your life, and he will give you many years in the land (Deut. 30:19).

Father,

I don't want to be a bitter woman. But sometimes relationships leave a sour taste, and I don't know what to do when everything within me wants revenge and payback. So now I submit myself to You and ask You, by the power of Your Spirit, to put within me the desire to walk in Your way and give all of my hurts to You—You can take charge of them. I also give all of "me" to You—and You can take charge of me. Make me a lover of You and a lover of people. Amen.

Journal Page

- What hurts have I internalized? For what hurts am I seeking payback? What hurts do I need to forgive?

_____

_____

_____

_____

_____

_____

_____

_____

_____

_____

_____

_____

_____

_____

_____

_____

_____

_____

_____

_____

_____

_____

_____

_____

_____

_____

KEY POINTS FROM LESSON 4

- The experience of being hurt, misunderstood, or wronged is a fact of life.
- We must admit our hurt to God for healing and direction.
- There is a war going on in the spiritual realm that threatens all good that can come from unity with others.
- We can grow bitter or better—it's a choice.
- Our response to our hurts can change our lives.
- God calls us to make every effort to live in unity.
- We are to seek to live at peace if at all possible.
- We must unpack the old self and attitudes of the past.
- We can embrace the Spirit's life within us.
- Forgiveness is part of the Jesus style.
- Forgiveness is an action that requires change in response to the one forgiven.

Living Forgiveness ... True Freedom

*As long as you maintain your own personal interests and ambitions, you
cannot be completely aligned or identified with God's interests.*

—OSWALD CHAMBERS

Love is never letting a problem to be solved become more important than a person to be loved.

"I will never forgive him!" Tears streamed down my new friend's face, falling onto her pale green sweater. I knew that though forgiveness was the last thing she wanted to face, it was the exact thing she finally needed to face—head on with Christ.

Forgiveness is a word that plants fear into the hearts of many people. We fear that if we forgive, we will be opening up ourselves for future hurt and mistreatment. Many of us feel that if we forgive others, it will be like letting them off the hook or giving them a stamp of approval for the way they have wronged us.

Even Christians feel this way, and we struggle to believe that it is okay to let go and let God be God in all areas of our lives. Unfortunately, what we fail to recognize is that when we as Christians insist on not forgiving, we are not living in God's best purpose for our lives. By not letting someone off the hook, we are actually snagging ourselves with that same hook and breeding bitterness, resentment, and all kinds of ugly things in our own hearts.

When bitterness reigns in our lives, we become negative, critical women. This kind of woman is not what God intended when He created us and when He forgave us in our own sinfulness. In many churches this type of person is the norm. Sadly, we have become accustomed to judging one another harshly for every poor performance.

God in His grace forgives us time and time again. Some of us have done ugly, hideous things, yet

God forgives us over and over. Some of us have hearts full of deceitfulness and pride, yet God keeps loving us and working with us. One aspect of God's love toward us is forgiveness. And He has clearly told us that we are to love as He has loved us (John 15:12). This is hard, if not impossible, in most cases. But with God all things are possible, and in Him we have strength for all things (Luke 1:37; Phil. 4:13).

In this lesson we will look into God's Word and see what God's plan of forgiveness is for us in our relationships with other people.

 DAY ONE: RED LETTER LIVING

1. Read Matthew 6:1–15.

These are the words of Christ. Jesus is telling us some important life principles in this passage. We need to make note of some key points.

- We are not to do the right things for the sake of appearance and to please others. (What does Jesus call those who do this?)
- We are to remember that our heavenly Father sees all things, even those things done in secret. We are to do all things unto Him, out of a heart of love for God.
- We are to pray for God's will daily.
- We are to seek forgiveness from God for our sins, and we are to seek to forgive others as well.
- If we do not forgive, God will not forgive us.

- How do you respond to the idea that God won't forgive you if you don't forgive others?

2. Write out Matthew 6:14–15.

Forgive here in the Greek (*aphiemi*) can be translated as follows: forsake, lay aside, leave, let go, let alone, omit, yield up, put away. This definition speaks something powerful to me.

If I let go of the terrible things that someone has done to me, God will also let go of my offenses. Letting go means that I will choose to lay the offense aside and give it to God. Then God, who sees in secret and knows my heart, will honor me with the blessing of forgiving me, too.

If I choose instead to hold on to the awful things done to me, then I will be guilty of not obeying the will of God. Instead, I will be holding tightly to my own will—my own hurts and my own perceived rights. When I live as one not yielding my life situations to my heavenly Father, I am setting myself up for pain and separation from God.

My God knows and sees all things; therefore, I must live to please Him. If instead of pleasing God, I choose to please myself by nursing a grudge, I will also be choosing the consequences of that grudge. (Grudges happen when we don't let go of wounds.) Besides driving myself crazy with ugly thoughts and feelings, the worst consequence of my lack of submission to God and His Word is that I will not be forgiven for the wrongs that I commit.

• What does the Lord's Prayer, as outlined in Matthew 6, say to you on a personal level?

To forgive is also translated as *yield up*. It is important for us to realize that in our natural selves we will have a very hard time forgiving someone who has hurt us. Sometimes we have a hard time forgiving someone even the smallest offense. This is why it is important that we are aware that when God asks us to do something, His grace will enable us to carry it out. We must get in the habit of yielding up our hurts and offenses to God. Our Father who sees in secret will speak to the places in our hearts that need the strength of God in order to obey His Word. He will also give us personal and practical applications and steps to take in each individual circumstance. When—and *if*—we yield to God.

3. Read Luke 6:37–38. What are the key points?

Father,

It's the hardest thing to let go and forgive. Teach me to live by the measure of love You use. May I give out of that measure freely and willingly. Create in me a heart of submission toward Your will for me in my relationships. Amen.

 DAY TWO: A NEW SUBMISSION

1. Read James 4:6–10.

• What does God give you?

• What are three things you are to do (vv. 7–8)?

1.

2.

3.

• What does "humble yourselves before the Lord" mean to you in the area of forgiving others for the things they have done to hurt you?

• Write out the dictionary definition of *humble*.

In the Greek translation of James 4:10, *humble* means to bring ourselves low in the condition of our heart before God, to abase ourselves before God. One of the definitions in my dictionary reads, to take down a peg. I like that because that's exactly what I need to do in order to forgive someone. I must first get humble before my God—take myself down a peg—and look at the Lord God, His Word, and His ways. Then I can submit myself to His power and His Word. Without this first step of humbling myself before almighty God, I just might think someone actually owes me.

I find it quite interesting that the Bible tells us that the condition of our hearts should be to lower ourselves. The world says we are to elevate ourselves. Part of the reason it is so hard for us to let go and yield to God is because it has become unnatural for us to do so. The natural thing for us to do is to repay someone who has wronged us. We live in a get-in-your-face society. Sometimes we just want people who have hurt us to taste the pain we have tasted because of the way they mistreated us or those we love. But in yielding to what comes naturally, we set ourselves up for more pain. We do need, however, to confess the natural us to God (the us He already knows). When our hearts are laid open before Him, and we are no longer stuffing and brooding, we can instead begin confessing and be cleansed. Then we are in position to learn what it means to walk in the Spirit rather than in the old natural patterns of our flesh.

Remember that God is love. He loves us and doesn't require anything of us that will ultimately harm us. His requirements bring us to a place of more wholeness and more peace. Everything we are looking for can be found in our Savior and His ways for our lives.

2. Read Matthew 18:21–35.

• According to this passage, how many times did Jesus say we are to lay aside an offense and forgive? What is His point?

• Do you ever tire of the same people doing hurtful things in your life? Explain.

• Do you tire of someone doing the same thing over and over? Describe one specific example.

The key that opens the door to the locked rooms of our hearts is forgiveness. It is only when we have experienced forgiveness (and I cannot emphasize strongly enough that I am not talking about the simple nodding of one's head to a preacher's words; I mean being overwhelmed by the reality of forgiveness, being able to touch, taste, and smell its results) that we find the locks are sprung, the doors flung open, the windows tossed high, the rooms inhabited, and fires lighted on the hearths. It is then we discover that our hearts are finally free to love. They have become what the Creator intended them to be, places with immense capacity to embrace. We may even hear ourselves saying with surprise, "Do you know, there isn't anyone I can't love!" Then we will discover that God had done his work in us.[1]

—KAREN BURTON MAINS

It is a natural response to rise up in self-defense when someone hurts us. But just because it's natural to get defensive doesn't mean it's what is best for us. What's natural to us is usually just what is comfortable to our flesh or a pattern we have been taught to live by. As Christian women we are moving on to live in the Spirit, and what was once normal to us may suddenly be the opposite of what God is calling us to live in now.

• According to Matthew 18:21–35, what did Jesus tell Peter to do when his friend or brother sinned against him?

• What about the person who just keeps on making the same mistake?

• Have you ever been like the wicked servant, wanting to squeeze out every bit of repayment from someone who unjustly wronged you? If so, briefly describe a situation.

Most of us can handle relationships when things are going well. We have no trouble responding to people who are being nice to us and who are meeting our expectations. It's when they don't do what we think is acceptable that we lose our composure and often resort to acting according to our natural flesh. We want to throw people in prison—the prison of revenge and hurt. But when we forgive, we set the prisoner free. One of the definitions of forgive is *to give up wanting payback*. To forgive is to unlock the prison door and let the offender go free. But actually the person we end up freeing the most is ourselves.

> *"I have no choice." I often hear these words when someone is describing a painful situation in his life. Usually, the person sees himself as a helpless victim of evil persons or circumstances. In addition, depression, despair, and doubt characterize this thought life. Perhaps most damaging is a profound sense of powerlessness coloring his perspective. May I lovingly remind us that the powerless perspective is diametrically opposed to the Gospel of Jesus Christ? We possess incredible potential for choice and change! Why? Because the person who spoke the universe into existence offers to live within our beings. He has given us the power to choose Him as Lord of our entire lives, thus releasing new possibilities, perspectives, and power. And most amazing of all, this power to choose is available to every person! No exceptions! THE CHOICE IS OURS.[2]*
>
> —STEVE BEARDEN

3. Write out 1 Corinthians 13:5. (Remember that the word *it* refers to *love.*)

• According to this verse, what four things are the opposite of God's love?

1.

2.

3.

4.

Make note of the fact that love does not keep record of wrongs. We are to forgive over and over if that is what it takes. We can only do this when our eyes are fixed on Jesus and we are lined up with the desires of the Holy Spirit. Forgiveness is a process of the heart. God is interested in our hearts being yielded over to Him. Sometimes it doesn't feel at all black and white. In these times, we need to work through the gray areas with God—He will be faithful to lead us to the truth of forgiveness and love.

Father,
Your Word says You oppose the proud and give grace to the humble. May I lay myself before You daily and put stop signs up when pride creeps in. Amen.

   DAY THREE: PATTERNS FOR NEW LIVING

1. Read Colossians 3 (the rules for holy living).

• According to Colossians 3:5, what in your life needs to die?

• Put a checkmark by the following descriptions that apply to your earthly nature.
   ❑ having to have my own way
   ❑ being unwilling to obey God
   ❑ seeking revenge and repayment
   ❑ harboring anger, rage, and malice

• In what is the new self being renewed (v. 10)?

- What does Colossians 3:12–17 say to you about your relationships with others?

- What do these verses say you are to clothe yourself in?

- Where do you get these new garments?

- Write out Colossians 3:13. Memorize this verse!

Forgiveness is lining up your will with God's Word and will. It is saying, "Thy will be done!" No one ever feels like forgiving. We cannot wait until we *feel* like forgiving. We usually aren't jumping for joy or ready to do things that are hard. We must acknowledge that we can forgive with God's strength, power, and love. We make the choice to obey God, and He provides the power to complete the work. He does in us what we could never do ourselves.

> So, chosen by God for this new life of love, dress in the wardrobe God picked out for you: compassion, kindness, humility, quiet strength, discipline. Be even-tempered, content with second place, quick to forgive an offense. Forgive as quickly and completely as the Master forgave you. And regardless of what else you put on, wear love. It's your basic, all-purpose garment. Never be without it (Col. 3:12–14 MSG).

Father,
I cannot wait for feelings to dictate faith. I must live by faith, and faith in Your love for me and Your desire for me to love others. Give me the freedom to live in this truth. Amen.

DAY FOUR: FREEDOM FROM HOLDING OTHERS HOSTAGE

1. Write out the following verses.

Psalm 17:10

Ephesians 4:18

• Has your heart become callous because of an offense suffered? If so, how do you think it happened?

> *In fact our recovery and well being is intimately tied to our forgiveness of others. It does no good to receive grace with one hand, and deal out judgment with the other (Matthew 18:21–35). We need to forgive not just with our will but from the "heart," from our whole being. Forgiveness is a deeply emotional process whereby we deal with all our feelings. We must be honest about our hurt and anger and not close our hearts and become callous.[3]*
>
> —HENRY CLOUD AND JOHN TOWNSEND

2. Read 1 Corinthians 10:13.

• Are you tempted today with unforgiveness? If so, why?

• What does 1 Corinthians 10:13 promise you?

On a piece of paper make a list of those whom you are holding captive in your mind due to the ill feelings of hurt, anger, or unforgiveness. If necessary, you may find it helpful to write a letter to each of these people. This letter will never be sent; it is for your healing and cleansing. Once the letter is written and your frustration is out in the open, pray. Then take your list and your letters and rip them up, burn them in a fireplace, or find another way to discard them. This is symbolic of how you are handing these people and their offenses over to God. They are in God's hands. He has provided a way of escape, and it is the love of Jesus.

It is God's will that you forgive your offenders; therefore, when you strongly do not want to act according to God's will, you are being tempted to follow your sinful human flesh, obeying the natural way of responding and doing things. If we are going to be lifted to new heights, we must follow God and obey His Word. It is an act of will and an act of choice, but the carrying out of that choice is a miracle of His Spirit. He desires to grant you that power, that miracle, that wonderful ability to

- rise above,
- take the higher road,
- walk in the Spirit,
- turn the other cheek,
- allow God to handle the offender.

God provides a way out. His Word promises that.

Lord,
You know who I can't seem to let go of. I give those relationships to You here and now. Amen.

DAY FIVE: WALKING IN THE REALITY OF TRUTH

1. Read Ephesians 4:30–32.
- According to these verses, what grieves the Holy Spirit?

- What are you to get rid of?

- How are you to live?

2. Read Luke 6:27–38.

An enemy is anyone you are at odds with today, a hostile force, power, or person. According to this passage, we are to do these four things in our relationships:

- love
- bring good to
- bless
- pray for

- Does this just apply to the good relationships? Explain. (See Luke 6:32.)

- How are you to treat those who actually hate you or cause you pain (Luke 6:28)?

- Is this an impossible command or challenge? Why, or why not (Phil. 4:13)?

- In which of your relationships can you begin applying God's Word today?

- We often are judgmental toward the difficult people in our lives. What does Luke 6:37 say we are not to do to these people?

I am not to ...

I am not to ...

- What two things in Luke 6:37–38 are you to do in your relationships?

- Will you be blessed if you follow in God's ways? How?

Pray this week for each person you have had a difficult time loving or forgiving. Ask God to forgive you for holding on to the offense instead of yielding it up to Him. Pray according to God's Word. Ask God by the power of His Spirit to give you practical ideas and insights unique to your individual situation that will help you step out in a love-walk. Now that you have forgiven, ask God to continue working in the deepest parts of you. Walk by faith now, not by sight or feeling.

Remember, this does not mean you will forget the offense. You cannot forget a rape, murder, abuse, divorce, adultery, theft, etc. But, the memory of an offense can lose its power, and the circumstance that has caused you hurt can be covered in Christ.

Only the Spirit of God could do such a wonderful work of grace and forgiveness in us. We just have to choose which direction we will go. To forgive or not to forgive is our decision. The choice we make determines the direction; God's grace and power determine the outcome.

We aren't aiming for a perfect performance, but we are making it our aim to be pointed in the right direction. In these situations the right direction is toward the heart of God and His Word. When we are pointed in the direction of love, God can and will do amazing miracles in our hearts.

Trials are not enemies of faith
but are opportunities to see
the faithfulness of God.

Father,

It is my heart's desire to walk worthy of the calling You have called me to. You have called me to be Your daughter, and now I want to live with Your eyes, seeing people the way You see them. I want to reflect the attitude and personality of my Father. And, I know that only You can do that perfect work in me. My part is to move closer to You through obedience, surrender, and humility. I am Yours, Lord … all that I am, all that I will ever be. Teach me how to live. Amen.

Journal Page

- Lord, the "enemy" I most need help in loving this week is …

KEY POINTS FROM LESSON 5

- Jesus gave His example for living in the red letters of the Gospels.
- We are not to live in the red letters for their sake, but to follow Christ's example.
- We are to forgive others as we want God to forgive us.
- We must learn to let go of hurts and give each hurt to the Lord.
- Our pride gets us into trouble, while humility promotes grace and wholeness.
- It is never God's plan for us to hold a grudge.
- We must take the higher road and not wait for others to do it first.
- We are to bring good to others, blessing them, loving them, and praying for them.

Living Mercy ... As He Is Merciful

LESSON 6

*Life is a process: a complex, ever-continuing, ever-changing set of
problems. The choice is not if you'll accept problems, but how.*
—TIM HANSEL

Mercy is kind and compassionate treatment, coupled with a disposition toward forgiveness.

To have a disposition of forgiveness means one has a habitual tendency toward forgiveness. Such a person is inclined to offer forgiveness when needed. This is someone who is kind, compassionate, and merciful. Sounds to me like a sketch of God! Kindness, compassion, and mercy are all characteristics of Jesus Christ. If we are serious about learning to follow Him, we must seriously desire to understand these traits.

 DAY ONE: GOD IS MERCIFUL

1. Write out the following verses.

Deuteronomy 4:31

Nehemiah 9:31

• What do these verses tell you about God?

2. Write out Ephesians 2:4–6.

• According to this passage, what have God's love and mercy done for you?

• Do you act as though you are in Christ? Explain.

3. Read Luke 6:32–36.

• What does Jesus instruct you to do in these verses that can be applied to your everyday life?

• What characteristic of God does Jesus tell you to imitate (v. 36)?

Lord,

Thank You for being a loving and merciful God. You love when I do not deserve to be loved. You show mercy when I am obstinate and disobedient. You are always calling me out and into Your love. I need to learn how to live with You as my Life, my Example, and my Guide to living with Your merciful heart toward others. Amen.

DAY TWO: LEARNING TO USE GOD'S MEASURE

1. Read Luke 6:37–38.

• A merciful person is someone who is Christlike—kind and forgiving. How does judging fit into the picture of a merciful person?

• Do you think someone oozing with mercy would be a critical and judgmental person? Why, or why not?

• What measure will be used to you? Why?

We live in a world of double standards. We judge others by a yardstick of perfect expectations, yet we don't want anyone using that same yardstick or pointing the same finger at us. We become negative and critical if others look at us the wrong way, but we don't want people scrutinizing how we are looking at them. This is a double standard. What we fail to realize is that if we are critical, judgmental, and unloving, it will come back to us later. It is the law of reaping and sowing, and it is as alive today as it has ever been.

2. Read Luke 6:41–42.

• What does this passage mean in your own words?

• Do you have trouble with pointing the finger or placing blame on others? If so, why do you think you struggle with this?

• Have you ever looked inside yourself, asking God to show you your own heart? If you have, what happened? If not, why not try it?

When you are pointing your finger at someone, you have three of your own fingers pointing back at you! Try it, you'll see.

It is amazing how we can quote verses such as Luke 6:41–42, but we do not live them. Mercy has not become a habitual part of our relationships. A merciful person is kind, compassionate, and eager to forgive!

3. Write out the following verses.
Matthew 12:7

1 Peter 1:3

4. Write out Isaiah 63:9 and circle key words in it.

Lord,
You desire that I walk in mercy more than You desire my sacrifice of doing "things" for You. The way I live toward others is important to You. Help me remember. Amen.

 DAY THREE: THE SACRIFICE OF MERCY

1. Write out Hosea 6:6.

2. Write out Matthew 9:12–13.

We can serve in church ministries until the Lord comes back and still not live as merciful people. One of the worst places for unkindness is right within the local church. This is a sad truth! We sacrifice our time, our money, and our lifestyles when in front of people, but what God really desires is that we love people. He desires mercy and not our sacrificial service that is laced with gossip, judgmental attitudes, and finger pointing. He desires that we walk in His love. That love hopes for the best in all people—the opposite of gazing at others with a critical eye. How do you treat others? Honestly. Remember, kind and compassionate treatment is a sign of a merciful heart.

3. Read Matthew 23:23–28.
- This is a very strong passage of Scripture, and these are the words of Christ. What three things did Jesus tell the Pharisees they had neglected (v. 23)?

1.

2.

3.

- What word does Jesus use to describe the Pharisees when they neglected these things?

Justice: fairness.
Mercy: kindness.
Faithfulness:
consistency with
the facts, steadfast
in nature.

Father,

I don't want to be a Pharisee. Clean me from the inside out. Clean the cup of my heart. Fill me with Your love, the promised love of God, and may mercy overflow from my cup each day. Amen.

 DAY FOUR: LIVING OUT OF A CLEAN CUP

1. How helpful for you is the cup-and-dish analogy in Matthew 23:25–26? Explain.

- Have you been guilty of being concerned only with appearances? Explain.

- Based on these verses, how do you suppose you obtain mercy to give to others?

2. Write out Lamentations 3:22–23.

It is because of God's mercy that we are not consumed. And each day we receive a new shipment of God's mercy and love. Do you suppose He can show you what it means to live in new mercies each day?

Some people have the mistaken idea that mercy is just the gift of caring and running around doing things for others. While doing these things is indeed kind and compassionate, it is not the essence of mercy. Mercy is an attitude of the heart. It is something that flows from the inside out. All believers can have mercy if they ask God for an internal overhaul. Mercy is part of God's nature, and therefore it is part of what He is making us to be.

3. Read James 4:1–4.

The battle is within us, and that is why the inside of the cup must be cleaned. If the inside heart is clean and the attitude in check, then the outside will sparkle with the beauty of mercy. But just as with anything else, we won't have mercy if we don't ask for it. Mercy is one of God's riches, and we can and should ask the Father to give us this wonderful attribute, because with mercy we can truly love others with the Father's love.

4. Write out the following verses.
Proverbs 11:17

Micah 6:8

Matthew 5:7

• What is the common theme here?

Lord,
May I be one who shows mercy! Teach me Your ways. Amen.

DAY FIVE: PUTTING ASIDE HUMAN WISDOM AND HUMAN LOVE

1. Read James 3:13–18.

• List the components of earthly wisdom.

• List the components of heavenly wisdom.

• Of what is heavenly wisdom full?

2. Read Matthew 5:1–9.

Mercy is a lot like forgiveness. If we show mercy, we too will receive mercy. You may not receive it today, but God's Word is true, and you will receive from Him what you have sown in others' lives. I think it is interesting that Jesus says peacemakers will be blessed and be called His children. He doesn't say the argumentative will be blessed. No. They are just doing battle and will pay for it in the end, either through circumstances or health issues. Being unkind, unforgiving, and unmerciful causes much stress to the mind and body. It is more work than it is worth but what comes naturally to most of us when we are crossed. Once we get it in our heads that God desires us to be merciful people and that He will provide the mercy we need, we can move forward by faith.

As my mother advanced in age, she needed help and care. She came to live with us in our downstairs bedroom. Many times I was frustrated with her. She had so many needs, and she seemed to be so demanding and negative. After a few years of this, I was becoming tired of taking care of her. It was then that I asked God to give me His heart of mercy toward my mother. The next day as I took her breakfast, I looked at her with different eyes. I gradually began to see some of the reasons she had fallen into the negative—her life had become painful and hard, and she didn't know how to grow old peacefully. I began to realize the frustration she felt because she had to be cared for as her health failed. Then I realized the need to look beyond myself and my past hurts or attitudes about her. It was my opportunity to be a vessel of love and mercy. I learned more from taking care of my mother in her last years than almost any single experience I have lived through. But I also realize that in order to show mercy, I have to always look at forgiveness. The following are some helpful areas to look at to be sure our hearts are clean and ready to show mercy in attitude and action.

I forgive people for all things they haven't done—

- for no phone calls when I was in great need
- for the lack of greeting and kindness, which seemed to be deliberate
- for not including me or inviting me
- for not encouraging me when I needed encouragement
- for not caring when it was in their power to care
- for withholding love

I forgive people the things that have been said—

- for the words that harmed me
- for the careless comments that cut through me
- for the pious phrases telling me how to improve myself when I thought I was trying already
- for the gossip aimed at me

I forgive people who have questioned my motives—

- for judging me
- for assuming the worst about me
- for pretending to like me while accusing me behind my back
- for saying I am prideful when I was doing my best to seek God for humility
- for lying about my motives based on their own baggage and assumptions

> I will give them singleness of heart and put a new spirit within them. I will take away their stony, stubborn heart and give them a tender, responsive heart (Ezek. 11:19 NLT).

Father,

All of these things I forgive that I may be forgiven. Through the act of giving these things to You, may my cup be cleansed, my heart made right, and my spirit ready to put others first, while committing myself to You. Amen.

Seeing my mother through different eyes began to change the way I treated her. I continued to pray for a heart of mercy for her, and the burden of her care seemed to lift from my heart. I realized I had an opportunity to be a channel of God's love to someone who was shut indoors and desperately needed cheer. As my attitude became more merciful, her attitude also changed. Then I realized being merciful to her was a good thing for me, too (Prov. 11:17).

• List some ways you can show mercy to the people God has placed in your life.

From the Heart

Mend a quarrel.

Search out a forgotten friend.

Dismiss a suspicion and replace it with a trust.

Write a letter to someone who misses you.

Encourage a youth who has lost his faith.

Keep a promise.

Forget an old grudge.

Examine your demands on others.

Fight for a principle.

Express your gratitude.

Overcome an old fear.

Take time to appreciate the beauty of nature.

Give God the praise.

Tell them again, and again, and again.

—AUTHOR UNKNOWN

A tender heart is a heart of mercy. Ask God for a new heart today. Ask Him by the power of His Spirit to fill you with His wonderful mercy.

Father,
I am limited within myself when it comes to mercy. But I come asking You to fill me with a merciful attitude toward the people You have placed in my life. May I learn to treat others with dignity and love. Give me a tender heart, one that looks beyond the natural and into the spirit of a person. I do want to walk in Your love and Your mercy. Teach me how to do this, show me the way. Amen.

> Surely goodness and mercy shall follow me all the days of my life (Ps. 23:6 KJV).

Journal Page

- God is getting down to the details with me, and He is saying …

KEY POINTS FROM LESSON 6

- God is a merciful God and treats us with compassion.
- As His, we are to treat others with the same compassion.
- Judging others keeps me from seeing them through Christ's eyes.
- When judging others, I too will be judged by God.
- God is more interested in how I treat others than He is interested in all the ministry I do.
- Pharisees have all the outward actions down pat but live with unclean hearts.
- Jesus desires to clean the cup of our hearts by the power of the Holy Spirit.
- Bringing my hurts to Jesus and allowing exposure of these hurts is a step toward loving others.
- Jesus can heal my heart, heal my painful memories, and change me.
- As God changes me, from the inside out, I am able to love and help others.
- Serving others is the hallmark of the Christian walk, provided it is done with a clean heart and right motive.

Living Kindness ... The Refreshed Life

LESSON 7

When God measures a man, He puts the tape around the heart instead of the head.[1]
—GOD'S LITTLE DEVOTIONAL BOOK

A generous man will prosper; he who refreshes others will himself be refreshed.
—PROVERBS 11:25

Kindness can be very practical and very spiritual. In this lesson we will look at both sides of kindness. Often we don't realize that how we live toward others affects our disposition toward life. Years ago I heard a speaker talk about living to be a blessing each day. She gave a challenge to try it—and so I did. The challenge was to look for people to be kind to, smile at, say an encouraging word to. Try it for one day, no matter what you are feeling like—try to be a blessing. At the end of that day take the temperature of your own attitude. You will be surprised to find that you feel better. Charles Stanley suggests four questions to ask God every day:[2]

1. What do You want me to do?
Ask the Holy Spirit to reveal to you specifically what He desires for you to do in any given day. Is there someone He desires you to contact? Is there someone He is planning to bring across your path? Is there a meeting you should attend or an appointment you should make?

2. How do You want me to act?
For everything that God desires to accomplish on this earth, He has a method He plans to use. What is the method He has set before you?

3. When do You want me to act?

We often fail because we get ahead of God or lag behind. For everything God desires to accomplish, He has a precise timetable. Ask the Holy Spirit to show you His schedule for your day.

4. How can I best represent You today?

Listen closely for God's answers to your questions. Some answers may come as you hear a Bible-based message, song, or conversation. Some will come from godly counsel. Others will come while you spend time in prayer and your heart is nudged to action.

 Day One: Imitating Christ

1. Write out Ephesians 4:32.

Kind: warm-hearted, friendly, generous with good will, pleasant, agreeable, accommodating.

We have looked at this verse several times in this study. That's okay, because repetition gives way to permanence in our hearts and minds, and this leads to a conviction that produces lifestyle change. This verse tells us there are three things that should characterize our relationships:

- kindness
- compassion
- forgiveness

Jesus Christ is all of these things in His relationship with us. He is the model of what a relationship should look like. We are imperfect people, and we have funny sin-based ideas of how we should treat people. Everything in our lives does not change overnight when we become Christians, but our spirit changes, that which we cannot see, promising us eternal life. Our natural self begins to change as we draw near to God, seek His ways, learn what His will is, and follow Him.

This explains why some Christians are mean, cranky, and not at all exemplifying those three attributes of kindness, compassion, and forgiveness. Why? Perhaps they have not been told about the lifestyle in which they would remain connected to Christ, receiving the flow of His love, His Spirit, and His wisdom into their practical life day by day. And, perhaps they did not realize that they were to take God's Word seriously in the practical applications of how to live out their lives.

Does this describe you?

When we do take God's Word as serious guidance, our lives change, our spirits soar, and we are lifted up out of the gunk we have been accustomed to dwelling in.

We have all grown up with patterns of how to treat people. Perhaps you did not like the way your parents or siblings acted, and you feel your actions now are much better than those of your family of origin. But are you looking to Jesus for the pattern of how to treat others? Don't look to the pattern of other people; look into the Word of Truth and find the pattern that will please God and bring freedom to your heart and relationships.

First Corinthians 13 says love is kind. This may be uncomfortable for you. In fact, this may be extremely uncomfortable for you. That's okay. God's Word is often uncomfortable for us to follow. We usually are living contrary to His Word because we haven't learned what it means to walk in the Spirit. When we walk in the Spirit we do not fulfill the ugly stuff of the flesh. Kindness is walking in the Spirit.

2. Write out Ephesians 5:1–2.

• According to these verses, whom are you to imitate?

• What describes God's attitude toward you?

• How are you then to live?

People who live long lives together eventually begin to sound alike, to talk alike, even to think alike. As we walk with God, we take on His thoughts, His principles, His attitudes. We take on His heart.[3]

—MAX LUCADO

To imitate means to mimic. We are to mimic or copy the patterns of Jesus. But God's Word never directs us to rely on our own power for effective change. We are to obey God, follow after His pattern, and pray for Him to do the work of Christ deep within us. I have heard it said that this is like praying toward heaven and rowing toward shore! We actively seek to walk in His ways and obey His precepts, but we are first actively praying for God to do His work in us.

3. Write out Ephesians 5:8–10.

See the difference here? The Bible says that you were dark and now you are light. Far too often we live in the dark in our dealings with others. We are to find out *what pleases the Lord* and remain there.

4. Write out Ephesians 5:15.

• What does this verse tell you about how you should live?

5. Read James 1:5. How do you become wise?

Lord,

You are my standard. In a world where there are many imitations, You are the real deal—for You are the God who created all. In a world where there are many ideals to copy and model, I choose to model my life after You. You, Jesus, are my life. I submit to Your standard. Amen.

 DAY TWO: CONFLICT HAPPENS

1. Read James 3:13–18.

• If you are receiving wisdom from God, how will your actions change?

• Will you think you are superior spiritually? Why, or why not?

• Are envy and selfishness spiritual? Why, or why not?

• What else will be present when there is bitter envy and selfish ambition in your life?

• What characteristics will you begin to take on when you are walking in the wisdom and will of God?

• Do you like the idea of being a peacemaker? Why, or why not?

Right about now you might be thinking, *But what about the difficult people in my life?* Good point! Let's see what God says about dealing with the difficult people and circumstances in our lives.

WHEN PEOPLE DON'T ACCEPT YOU

2. Read Matthew 10:11–14.

• Jesus was giving His disciples instruction for their ministry trip. He knew some people would not accept them or help them in any way. What did He tell the disciples to do when they were not welcomed?

Notice that He did not tell the disciples to defend themselves, explain themselves, argue their point, or spend days in endless discussions about why they should be welcomed. No, Jesus instructed the disciples simply to go on their way with no worry about the people who didn't want to have anything to do with them. The disciples were to shake the dust off their feet and leave those people to God without the arguments and hard feelings that are so prevalent in relationships and churches today.

• What does the saying "I agree to disagree" mean to you?

3. Continue reading in Matthew 10:17–20.

In this passage Jesus gives the disciples instruction for their pending persecution. Though most of us will not experience flogging or this type of persecution, there is an important attitude here that we can apply to our situations.

Do not worry.

The Spirit will speak through you.

In this life we will be faced with trauma in relationships. Our relationships are plagued with selfishness. We will have to walk into situations where we will not know what to say. We will not know what key will unlock the misunderstanding. That is why it is so important to stay close, connected, in tune, grafted in, surrendered, sold out, and submitted to the Father.

As we walk in the Spirit, we will be in tune with the Spirit, and that same Spirit will speak through us according to the wisdom of God, which by the way is peaceable!

4. Read Galatians 5:16–26.

• What is in conflict within you (vv. 16–17)?

• What are the human characteristics that damage relationships (vv. 19–21)?

• What are the characteristics of the Spirit that give new life to relationships (vv. 22–23)?

• With whom are you to keep in step (v. 25)? Why?

• If you were to take just this passage seriously, how would it change any of your current dealings with people?

Lord,
Help me to realize that conflict is part of life. Teach me to handle conflict without inflicting harm or making it worse than it has to be. Teach me Your way in dealing with others. Amen.

D{4}L | Day Three: Handling Anger

1. Read Matthew 18:15–17.

• What are you to do if someone sins against you?

• Whom is the conversation to be between?

• What if the person does not listen to you?

Too many times, especially as women, we go around the block several times with a problem before taking it to the person involved. This is gossip and tale-bearing. Ouch! When you have a problem, as uncomfortable as it might seem, take it directly to the source, and follow the way of the Word:

• Speak the truth in love.

• Have kindness on your tongue.

Let's look more closely at the things that may come naturally to us but damage our relationships: hatred, anger, resentment, and bitterness.

Hatred: animosity and hostility

Hatred doesn't happen overnight. It is what happens when you aren't dealing correctly with a problem when it first hits the scene, or when your pent-up stuff hits the fan! You were wronged; you became angry. What did you do with that anger? Did you allow it to fester into true hostility? Not a pretty sight, is it?

Anger: a strong feeling of displeasure, becoming mad or irate

Anger is a normal human emotion. Not everything in your life will please you, and not every person in your path will either. You will never be completely free of this emotion in this life. Things will happen to make you angry. The feeling of anger isn't wrong—it is what you do with anger that counts.

Let's look at God's way of handling anger.

A gentle answer turns away wrath, but a harsh word stirs up anger. (Prov. 15:1)

Ever notice how a harsh word seems to stir up your defense mechanisms? Someone has wronged you, and everything within you wants to scream at that person or at someone else who is available! At the moment the matchstick of anger is lit, you can choose to fight back and fan the flame, or you can trust God with the circumstance and handle the conflict in a healthy way. The beginning of Proverbs 15:1 states, "A gentle answer turns away wrath...."

Often we rage when someone has wronged us. We give full vent, because (we justify) this person deserves a piece of my mind, and he or she will not walk on me! According to Scripture this is how a fool deals with anger.

In contrast, when we are filled with God's wisdom, we will keep the anger in control. We will not deny the anger or the problem that caused it, but instead we will

- speak the truth in love (Eph. 4:15);
- deal with the problem humbly (Eph. 4:2).

Remember to allow God to work. Everything doesn't have to be solved today.

2. Write out Psalm 4:4–5.

- What does this passage have to do with handling anger?

You will not become a bitter person if you deal with a problem and then close the book on it, only opening the book if the problem arises again, then dealing with it once again and moving on. In Psalm 4:4–5 we see the picture of someone going away alone to bed and dealing with anger by offering a right sacrifice to God—surrendering the heart to God's will. When we follow the psalmist's example, God can minister to us and help us deal with any mistreatment. Instead of calling on every friend, try calling on almighty God!

If you do not choose to move on, you give the devil a foothold in your life. A foothold means a position that provides a place for advancement.

3. Write out Ephesians 4:26–27.

You should memorize these two verses. I cannot tell you how the application of them is helping me. I recognize that I will have anger from time to time. That's normal, I've accepted that. But, now I keep

A fool gives full vent to his anger, but a wise man keeps himself under control (Prov. 29:11).

myself on a time clock, literally. It seems to me that my anger should not spill over into another day. Or, to break it down practically, once twenty-four hours have passed, I better move on! Sometimes I let myself stew a few hours, but because I know it is not good to hold on to these things, I work at giving them to God and moving on. If the angry thoughts come back to haunt me, guess what? I take them back to the Lord and humble myself before Him. Regardless of my feelings at this point I am to act appropriately, according to the Spirit, even if the other person is not. This is where kindness comes in!

Father,
Even though I feel angry at times, teach me how to handle my actions according to Your Spirit and not allow my emotions to run wild. Amen.

D{4}L DAY FOUR: JEALOUSY—THE KINDNESS KILLER

1. Read James 1:19–25.
• Why do you suppose James writes, "Take note of this" (v. 19)?

• What three things does James urge you to do in verse 19?

1.

2.

3.

2. Jealousy harms relationships. Write out Galatians 6:4.

We are not to compare ourselves with another person. We should write that one hundred times, like children who haven't learned a fine point in school—just kidding, but it wouldn't hurt. Women are so prone to competition and comparison, and these lead to jealousy or pride. Both wreck relationships and rob people of the ability to be kind. Jealousy is simply envy over something someone else has that we *think* we need but don't have. The emphasis is on *think,* because we are really okay and have just what we need, but we think we don't; therefore, we compare, complain, feel insecure, and get jealous. Jealousy is one of the works of the flesh.

3. Read 1 Corinthians 3:3–9.
• Write out 1 Corinthians 3:3.

We don't need to be jealous because God has a purpose for each person. Let's get a grip here! If I am not gifted in areas where you are, then I must accept that our gifts were assigned to us by God's will. Again, what we really need is more connection to Jesus, more faith, and more perspective on the big picture and His love for us as individuals. His love is kind, and we can learn to be kind to one

Kind: pleasant,
courteous,
respecting others,
honoring others,
blessing them.

another when we realize that no one is a threat to us, because God will accomplish all He has planned for our lives.

Let's look at what our relationships will have in them when we are in step with the Spirit. Turn to Galatians 5:22 again. Let's concentrate on part of the fruit of the Spirit: kindness.

4. Read Colossians 3:12–17.

• According to this passage, what are you to put on like clothing?

• Do you think this applies to everyone in your life, or just to the people you like? Elaborate.

5. Read James 2:1–9.

This passage speaks to treating rich and poor differently, but it makes the point that God has no favorites. We should not apply His teachings only to our friends or convenient people. We are to apply His Word to all people we come in contact with.

You will be surprised at what will happen when you act kindly to those who have hurt you. Act kindly just because it pleases the Father. Do it according to God's will and Word, and watch as you are filled with the fruits of righteousness. Peace will be yours and so will forgiveness and mercy. It will feel strange at first. But it is God's way.

Lord,
Teach me how to value the "me" that You see and made rather than comparing or competing with any other person. In the foundation of Your love for me, may I find stability in my relationships with others. Amen.

DAY FIVE: LEARNING TO LIVE IN PEACE

Today is a day for practical observation and application.

1. Read Hebrews 12:14–15 and 13:1. What key thoughts or words do you identify?

2. Journal your thoughts about what God has been saying to you about kindness throughout this lesson.

3. List some practical ways you can show kindness to someone today.

Here are some of the practical things on my list:
- smile
- hold my tongue
- speak pleasantly
- listen
- ask questions about the person's life
- bake cookies
- send a card
- buy a gift
- say a prayer

- give a hug
- do someone else's chore
- be helpful
- smile again
- do not judge the person
- accept your differences
- do not compete with another person
- give the other person space
- find out what this person really needs and provide it (a night out, a car wash, etc.)
- pick up the phone and say hello
- send flowers
- extend respect and courtesy even to someone who dislikes me

Choosing not to sweat the small stuff, accepting another, warts and all—that is kindness. Remember: "Love is a God-given opportunity to refresh and encourage another." Be on the lookout for those God-given opportunities!

Father,

Many times I am just not kind at all. I want my own way; I am grumpy, moody, or irritable; and I just don't feel like being kind. After all, many people aren't kind to me either. But I realize that You have something better for me than living in the immaturity of my childish ways. I am just a child when I withhold kindness from another person. Today, may I smile more, and may I be more aware of what it means to be kind. Give me the grace to deal with anger as it comes up and teach me Your way of handling conflict. Amen.

Journal Page

- How could living in kindness refresh your life?

KEY POINTS FROM LESSON 7

- Being kind toward others is part of the Christ life.
- When we are kind, we ourselves are filled and refreshed.
- As believers, we are to copy Christ.
- Kindness, compassion, and forgiveness are the Jesus style.
- When we go to God's Word for wisdom, we change.
- It is okay for people to be different from us. This doesn't have to affect our attitude toward them.
- As we walk in the Spirit, kindness is one of the outcomes of our actions.
- Conflict is part of life. Drama is our doing.
- Jealousy kills relationships.
- Kindness builds relationships.
- Kindness is our new clothing to put on as believers.

Living Real ... The Practical Side of Love

LESSON 8

The deep waters of the Holy Spirit are always accessible, because they are always flowing. Will you claim afresh and anew today to be immersed and drenched in these waters of life? [1]

—L. B. COWMAN

Love is proven by actions.

Practically speaking, love isn't love if it is in theory only. We can talk about love and its attributes, but if love is not in our lives at the down-to-earth, rubber-meets-the-road level, then we are just all talk. This is exactly what non-Christians often complain about when asked about Christians. They think we are hot-air hypocrites.

This is an unfortunate judgment, because non-Christians don't always practice everything they preach either. The best thing I ever heard said about our actions is this: Preach Christ always; use words when necessary.

We are to live the love of God, not just talk about it. We seem to know a lot in our heads, but we do not see the evidence of the things we know practiced on the daily, real-life level. When you meet Christians who are practicing what they believe to be God's way, it is refreshing and exciting. It gives us hope that the Spirit of Christ can become a part of our lives on a practical level.

Well ... guess what? Jesus wants to be very much a part of your life on a practical level too. He wants to make you a vessel of His awesome and magnificent love, poured out to everyone you come in contact with. Does this mean you are sickeningly sweet? No, no, no. It means you are passionately surrendered to the outpouring of His Spirit. He will make His work in you very, very practical.

DAY ONE: FAITH WITHOUT WORKS IS NOTHING

Practical: serving
a purpose, useful,
practice, use
rather than theory
or speculation,
sensible, functional,
handy.

1. Read James 2:14–17. What is this passage saying to you?

2. Read Matthew 25:31–40.

• Where do you see the practical side of love here?

• Do you walk away from the hungry in your life? If so, what keeps you from giving the practical things they need?

• What are the action parts of this passage?

• Do these passages from James and Matthew contradict the Bible's teaching that we are saved by grace alone? Explain.

Jesus was teaching that everything we do, we do for Him. Not just acts of worship, church services, or evangelistic ministries, but even the everyday practical things. Feeding someone, meeting a need for someone, visiting someone who needs a visitor—all these things are very down-to-earth practical things. And each of these things represents the practical side of our spirituality. These things are the deeds that must accompany our faith in order for us to live out our faith in this world we live in.

3. Read on in Matthew 25:41–45. This is a picture of faith in actions, not words. What is this saying to you about your life?

Father,
I desire to learn what it means to apply faith in Your word of truth to my everyday life and relationships. Teach me what this means. Amen.

DAY TWO: GOD'S INSTRUMENT

> Vessel: a hollow utensil used as a container.

1. Read 2 Timothy 2:20–25.

In my office I have a few things that are meaningful to me. Some might wonder why I have certain little props in my sitting area. Above the small table that is surrounded with two chairs, hangs a beautiful picture. But it is not just a picture. At first glance it looks like a lovely Thomas Kinkade, but when you look closer, you see it's a Kinkade puzzle with all the intricate pieces neatly glued into one beautiful work of art. This is my reminder of Romans 8:28.

On the table under the picture there is a very small wrapped gift. The gift reminds me that each day is a gift and that I need to present my life daily to Jesus for His use. Finally, there is a miniature metal pitcher. A simple metal pitcher, empty and with no decorative touch. This reminds me that God desires to pour through my life as His vessel, His little pitcher. I need to remain the empty vessel through which He may pour His love, His grace, His kindness, and His mercy to others.

Sometimes I just look inside the empty pitcher and remind myself that Jesus wants me emptied of self so that I will not taint the work of His Spirit.

• Jesus has called each of us to be an instrument of noble purposes. According to 2 Timothy 2:20–25, what are the things He says He will do in us? He will make us

1.

2.

3.

• What clear instruction does verse 22 give?

flee evil _____

pursue _____

pursue _____

pursue _____

pursue _____

• Look up the word *pursue* and write down the definition.

To pursue righteousness means that you are seeking to please God and pursue anything and everything that will make your walk pleasing to God. Part of pursuing righteousness, faith, love, and peace is keeping track of our tongues.

• According to verses 23–25, what should you not do?

2. **One practical way to show others the love of God is to speak kindly of them. Look up the following verses and write out the one that is most meaningful to you. Then commit it to memory this week.**

Proverbs 11:13

Proverbs 16:28

Proverbs 26:20

Lord,
Work in me kindness of thought, tongue, and action. Amen.

 DAY THREE: DON'T GRUMBLE OR YOU WILL BE JUDGED

1. **Read Hebrews 11.**
- According to this chapter, what practical things did the men and women of old do?

- How did they live?

2. **Write out Hebrews 10:28.**

Imagine your name in this verse. I can read it this way: "Debbie will live by faith, and if she shrinks back from that faith, God will not be pleased with her."

I want God to be pleased with me—that is my life's goal. I desire to know Him more and more and to live a life pleasing to Him. When I do certain actions by faith, God is pleased. When I shrink back because of my own fear or my own flesh, He is not pleased with my choice to do so.

Remember that sometimes you have to act out love, and part of that is doing those things that are scriptural for you to do. Don't wait to *feel* anything. That isn't faith! Anyone can love and do practical acts of kindness and love without feeling warm and fuzzy toward the person. When you feel empty, yet you still walk in love according to God's Word, you please Him. It is then that God's love can break through you.

3. Write out Hebrews 13:15–16.

- Through whom are you to live and love? What does this mean?

- What are you not to forget?

- What do you think the word *sacrifice* means here?

Sacrifice: forfeiture of something valuable for the sake of something else.

Doing good to others is somewhat of a sacrifice, isn't it? You have to forfeit your own feelings sometimes, giving those feelings to God and believing by faith that He will cause you to love other people His way. It is also a sacrifice for us when we are tired, sick, busy, or emotionally spent. Some women suffer great hormonal swings, and any act of kindness they make might be through gritted teeth. Nevertheless, we are to offer God this sacrifice, obeying His will and living His Word out in practical ways.

Father,
Teach me the value of heart sacrifice, the surrender of my actions, and the yielding of my attitudes and moods to You. Amen.

 Day Four: A Reality Check

1. **Take a personal inventory of the people in your life with whom you have unfinished business. You cannot change other people, but you can submit yourself to God. After each name, jot down ideas of things you can do for these people as practical ways to live out your faith despite their actions.**

Let us live in the light of love by faith! Each day everything we do has an impact. Let's make it our goal to leave the heartprint of Jesus on everything and everyone we touch today. Remember, we are only responsible for our actions, not another's response. Let the Spirit fill you and flow through you to others as you live in kindness and love as His everyday vessel. Loving God and others is real and practical—let's live in the practical side of love.

2. **Read James 4:1–3. What happens to destroy fellowship? Describe the process.**

But you are a chosen people, a royal priesthood, a holy nation, a people belonging to God, that you may declare the praises of him who called you out of darkness into his wonderful light (I Peter 2:9).

When we cling to selfish ambitions, the battles within us cause us to struggle with others. We want our way, we don't get it, the claws come out, and we get ugly.

3. Read James 4:7–10. What do we do to keep ourselves free from the selfishness that destroys our fellowship with God and others?

Staying humble before the Lord is key. Staying connected with the Father is a key. It is not an emotional state—it is a state of obedience.

Lord,
In relating to others, help me to be humble and put others first. Amen.

 DAY FIVE: LIVING OUTSIDE THE BOX

1. Read James 4:11–12 and 5:9.
- What do these verses say about judging your neighbor?

- Do you ever fall into the trap of slandering another person and maybe justifying your actions with some Christian cliché, such as, "I'm only telling you so that you can pray"? What would James say about that? Why?

- What about grumbling? Grumbling is that under-the-breath, exasperated, "I'm trying not to say it, but it just keeps slipping out" stuff. What does James 5:9 say about this?

• How does keeping our mouths shut encourage fellowship to grow?

Keeping our mouths shut is very hard for us as women, but it is something we need to set our hearts toward. We should not give ourselves the liberty to judge, grumble, or otherwise slander another person. In Christ we can do all things, and sometimes that "thing" is keeping our mouths shut!

2. Read James 3:3–12. Write down what this passage is saying to you about your mouth and how you speak of others.

3. Read Proverbs 6:16–19.
• In your own words, what are the seven things the Lord hates?
1.

2.

3.

4.

5.

6.

7.

• God hates when we do things that promote the disunity of our fellowship. How does this apply to your situation today?

4. Read Proverbs 6:20–23. What do these verses say to you about the importance of God's Word?

5. Read Matthew 18:15–17. This is the second time we've looked at this passage. How is it relevant to the practical love we've been talking about in this lesson?

• What is the end result of our fellowship with a person if there is no resolution from the process Matthew 18:15–17 describes?

This act of cutting someone off is not to be done in a hurtful manner. If you cannot find resolution, then give this person over to the Lord. Let God work. Do not try to help God by gossiping, having slanderous conversations, or trying to win people to your side. Those are immature and show you are insecure. Don't throw away your confidence in God. Trust God. You should treat this person as an acquaintance with respect and courteous kindness. This person is God's child. Remember that!

6. Read Ephesians 5:29–32.

This passage describes fellowship. Marinate in this passage. Read it over and over. Building each other up causes fellowship to grow and pleases God.

Find out what the will of the Lord is, what pleases Him, then GO!

HeartPrints
Whatever our hands touch—
We leave fingerprints!
On walls, on furniture,
On doorknobs, dishes, books.
There's no escape.
As we touch we leave our identity.

O God, wherever I go today
Help me to leave heartprints!
Heartprints of compassion
Of understanding and love.
Heartprints of kindness
And genuine concern.
May my heart touch a lonely neighbor
Or a runaway daughter
Or an anxious mother
Or perhaps an aged grandfather.

Lord, send me out today
To leave heartprints.
And if someone should say,
"I felt your touch,"
May that one sense Your love
Touching through me.[2]

—RUTH HARMS CALKIN

Father,

I desire to leave Your heartprints everywhere I go. May my life be an encouraging word to a discouraged person. May I be open to Your leading as You shape me into a vessel for Your use. I ask You to use me today and every day, according to Your power that is at work within me—the power of love. Amen.

Journal Page

• What comes to mind when you think of leaving "heartprints"? What are some that you can leave?

_____

_____

_____

_____

_____

_____

_____

_____

_____

_____

_____

_____

_____

_____

_____

_____

_____

_____

_____

_____

_____

_____

KEY POINTS FROM LESSON 8

- Love is not just a theory but is something we learn to practice daily.
- In order to love with *agapao*, we must be connected to Christ each day.
- *Agape* love is not just spiritual, it is shown in action, thus making it practical.
- Love without action is no love at all, just as faith without works is dead.
- We have the privilege of living as God's instruments in this world.
- Gossip kills.
- Love protects and shields.
- Our words are powerful, bringing life or death to our relationships.
- Doing good to others is not to depend on their doing good to us.
- Our actions toward others are to be from a single focus of Christ first.

Living Unselfishly ... Seeking Another's Best

LESSON 9

Many of us are drowning in our own emptiness, not realizing that this is an invitation to be filled by an ever-present God, a God who loves us more than we will ever understand or experience.[1]

—TIM HANSEL

... building others up according to their needs.

—EPHESIANS 4:29

Love is not a feeling. It is an overwhelming passion to help and bless and deliver and comfort and strengthen and give joy to others just as the Lord Jesus always did.

Living to seek another's best is living as God's everyday vessel. Often we try to do what's best for someone else but end up feeling frustrated because we have been unsuccessful at meeting his or her need. It is important that we recognize we must first seek God before we can seek to be a blessing of God to another person. If we are not seeking God and are not in fellowship with Him, we will not deliver the things only God's Spirit knows another person needs. We will be delivering our own goodwill, but that goodwill runs short and empties out over time. Our own goodwill gets frustrated when unrecognized, and then the whole vicious cycle of relational problems begins again.

When we are operating out of God's resource of love, we trust that He is using us as His vessel. He will give us the wisdom and grace to display just the right touch that the receiver needs at the time. When we are not recognized for the good deeds, we will dismiss it, knowing that we are asking God to love through us and the outcome is His business. In other words, when we do things God's way, seeking first His kingdom, we will have peace and all the things we need will be added to us as we serve Him.

Let's look at some relational roles we may fall into.

DAY ONE: EMPLOYEES AND EMPLOYERS

1. Read Ephesians 6:5–8. Write out verse 6.

It's hard to see the word *slave* and relate to it. But in our day these instructions apply to anyone who is working for another. According to this passage, we are to have certain attitudes toward our employers. They are

- respect
- fear (a reverent sort of fear)
- a sincere heart
- obedience to the employer's rules

Many people work in environments where the only thing they have is the obedience to the rules. They do not respect, honor, or have sincere hearts toward the one who is providing a job for them. There may be good reason for disrespect—maybe the employer is an overbearing lout! Now here comes the choice. As a Christian, you are to follow the example of Christ, who always put another first, knowing that God the Father would take care of Him. He was obedient to death on the cross; therefore, even if you don't agree with everything about your employer as a person, Scripture clearly outlines some things for you to do. They are

- obey (although not to the point of doing something illegal or immoral) and treat your employer with respect;
- serve wholeheartedly.

Remember who you are really obeying and serving.

- In what sense are you really the Lord's employee during that work shift? Why?

• What will the Lord do when you make this choice?

By giving your best work, you are seeking the best for your employer and also for the company. You are also lining yourself up with scriptural and spiritual principles.

2. Write out 1 Peter 2:18–19.

• Are you to respect even those who don't deserve it? Why?

The key element here is *being conscious of God*. There is that seeking-God concept again! The Bible is really so basic. We just somehow keep overlooking the basics.

• Why do you suppose so many of us have trouble following these instructions for employees? Do you suppose these truths are so simplistic that they seem impractical and therefore hard to follow?

3. Write out Ephesians 6:9.

Wow! Is this ever important to remember for those who are in authority over others! There is no favoritism with God. He loves all people the same, and there aren't different levels of people, just people that He created. Some people have a position of higher authority in this life, but that doesn't mean anything to God except that those people are to treat those under them with respect and serve them with a sincere heart, seeking their best.

This is a concept that has many rewards. If the employer or overseer is good to his or her people, then they will naturally want to please the employer by giving their best effort. As Christians, we need to be convinced that our best is always what we are called to give regardless of circumstances. The employer who looks out for the good of his or her employees will almost always be rewarded with respect and hard work. And if not—it's God's problem.

Lord,
I come to You with all my relationships and ask that You show me how to live as Your light and life in each one. Amen.

 DAY TWO: SHINING IN THE MARKETPLACE

1. Read 1 Peter 2:9–17 and write out verse 17.

"But I can't," you say. "I just can't live this good life!"

No kidding. Neither can I in my strength, and neither could the apostle Paul. Always doing the right thing goes against my ego and my natural tendencies. I am comforted that it's not just me, but everyone who struggles with this. Even the most spiritual-looking person (How do you "look" spiritual? I never have figured that out!) or the most pious-acting person struggles with *self*. Take Paul's word for it in the book of Romans.

> Friends, this world is not your home, so don't make yourselves cozy in it. Don't indulge your ego at the expense of your soul. Live an exemplary life among the natives so that your actions will refute their prejudices. Then they'll be won over to God's side and be there to join in the celebration when he arrives (1 Peter 2:11–12 MSG).

2. Read Romans 7:14–8:14. Can you identify with what Paul describes here—knowing the things you should not do, yet doing them anyway? If so, give an example that involves a relationship with another person.

• Write out Romans 7:18.

> *"I know that all God's commands are spiritual, but I'm not. Isn't this also your experience?" Yes. I'm full of myself—after all, I've spent a long time in sin's prison. What I don't understand about myself is that I decide one way, but then I act another, doing things I absolutely despise. So if I can't be trusted to figure out what is best for myself and then do it, it becomes obvious that God's command is necessary.*
>
> —ROMANS 7:14–16 MSG

• What do you think it means to be led by the Spirit of God?

• Do you want to be led by the Spirit of God in your relationships? Why?

Lord,

I desire to walk in Your Spirit. I am asking You to show me how. My personal relationships are the easiest target for my flesh and for misunderstandings. Teach me how to apply Spirit-led living to this most practical place. Amen.

DAY THREE: WALKING IN THE SPIRIT AT HOME

First Corinthians 13:5 says love is not self-seeking. If we are led by the Spirit of God into God's love, we will have relationships that are characterized by seeking another person's *best*.

1. Write out 1 Corinthians 10:23.

2. Write out Philippians 2:4.

3. Read Philippians 2:13–21.

I find it encouraging that it is God who works in me, to change my will to bring it in line with His! Philippians 2:13 has been my marinade over the past six months. What I mean by that is that I have been soaking in this verse for many months now. When I soak in a verse, it begins to sink into my thick skin and become part of the flavor of who I am. I have noticed that now when I am discouraged, I am more apt to remind myself that God is working in me to will and to do His good pleasure for my life. And when there is noticeable fruit (a miracle!), I can be excited that it is God working in me, bringing me in line with His plan and His design for me individually so that *He may be glorified*.

• We are to do everything without what? (See Phil. 2:14.)

• What do most people do (v. 21)?

• Do you think it is scriptural to look out for others? Explain.

We live in a "me first," "take care of #1" society. Because of this, it is hard to take the Word of God seriously, but we must purpose in our hearts not only to be a loving people but also to be a people who are unselfish and caring for others.

Now let's move from workplace to home. Even if you're not married, you probably have feelings about what the Bible says about marriage.

4. Read Ephesians 5:21–24, 32–33.

Submit? Is that a hard, ugly word to you? Did you know that one of the definitions of submit is *to be in consideration of someone else?* When picturing *submit* in today's terms, I see a used and abused wife, struggling for some individuality and identity, a servant to her husband's whims, desire, and commands. But actually this is not the scriptural focus of submission at all. Remember, God always works in our lives out of His love for us. Therefore, He always gives us directives that will be good for us and not harm us. We do not have to be afraid of God's will, nor do we have to be selective about what we will obey in His Word. If it is in His Word, it is always for our best. (Look at it this way: Jesus seeks our best all the time, and now we are learning that trait of seeking another's best.)

• Write out Ephesians 5:21.

Notice this verse says we are to submit to one another. This isn't just speaking about marriage—this is to be the norm in all relationships. Read Ephesians 5:15–21, and you can see this is talking about all human relations. We are to respect one another, being considerate of one another because we love God and want to please Him.

• Write out Ephesians 5:32–33.

The profound mystery is how God can take two lives and join them spiritually as one. This does not just describe marriage but also the mystery of our relationship with Jesus Christ. We are born into this world as flesh and are reborn by the Spirit of Christ, which makes us one with Him. This is a mystery. And just as Christ loves us, and we respect God and His ways, husbands are to love their wives, and wives are to respect their husbands. But what about the mean ones? What if my husband doesn't love me, or the Lord, or anything other than himself? We must go back to Ephesians 5:21.

> Out of respect for Christ, be courteously reverent to one another (Eph. 5:21 MSG).

Being courteous to your mate doesn't mean you always have to agree. It doesn't mean you can't give your opinion. It also doesn't mean that you should put up with abuse of any form. If you feel you are in an abusive situation, you should seek professional help. By the way, living with a husband who is less than perfect does not constitute abuse. If you are in actual abuse, you probably know it without anyone telling you. Remember, speaking up and getting help in an abusive situation could be seeking another's best. Sometimes people don't change because they aren't required to.

"We always hurt the ones we love" is an old saying that rings with truth. That is why we need to learn to walk in the Spirit and ask God by His power to teach us the walk of love with our mates. Seeking their best may be agreeing to that fishing trip or football game. Husbands need space too, and they need our love and support. Sometimes we get so bogged down with our responsibilities that we feel overwhelmed and forget that husbands get overwhelmed too. When was the last time you looked at your husband and actually tried on his shoes to see how you could best support him?

> Wives, understand and support your husbands in ways that show your support for Christ (Eph. 5:22 MSG).

Father,
You can change me—have Your way in me.
Amen.

 D{4}L   DAY FOUR: FAMILY TIES

Not all of us have husbands and not all of us have children. But enough of us do that these relationships deserve attention. Family can be the hardest ones to love well!

1. Read Colossians 3:21.

2. Read Proverbs 31:27–28. What happens when you are too hard on your children?

This passage shows us a picture of a woman who is living to seek the best for her family, and in the end the writer calls her blessed and praises her for all her love and attention.

You will teach your children *about* love *by* loving. Children learn more from our actions than our words. If I tell my children God is love, and they see me not loving, then they will get a mixed message. The powerful legacy God has given us to pass to our children is Jesus Christ and His love. We must be a loving people if the gospel is to have this impact. Remember, your choice today makes a ripple effect tomorrow.

3. Read Ephesians 6:2–3.

As adults we still have a responsibility to our parents. We are to honor them. This means we are to esteem, respect, and treat them kindly. And as in all other relationships, we are to seek their best.

• Ephesians 6:3 actually contains a promise. What is that promise?

This concept of honoring your parents may be hard to swallow. Your parents may be mean and, in your mind, undeserving of your honor. But what does Scripture say? What would Jesus do? What are you to do?
  • Give your attitude about your parents to Christ.
  • Pray for your parents.
  • Ask God by His Spirit to work in you His love for your parents.
  • By faith, act respectfully even before the feelings come.
  • Walk in kindness and honor as to the Lord.

Sometimes honoring your parents will mean honoring their wishes. For me, that has been a challenge at times. Both my sister and I wanted to honor our mom's wish to stay out of a nursing home. We set our hearts to do whatever we had to do to take care of a sick, elderly parent. It wasn't easy. Sometimes we just had to do what was right by faith alone. And always we had to pray and ask God to love her and take care of her through us.

We are imperfect daughters but He is a perfect God, and we want to take on His characteristics. This was our prayer while our mother was alive. I know I can speak for my sister in saying that we both now see that the time with our mother was a gift to us. It changed us, stretched us, caused us to grow. Most of all, it gave us a different love for our mother and healed old wounds. We have no regrets. In taking care of her, we have been blessed.

Do you have aging parents? Do you look for ways to honor them and seek their best interest? A visit would be nice, and so would cards, regular phone calls, and especially regular prayer. How do you wish to be treated when you are old? Think about it, and treat your parents with the same tenderness, kindness, and respect. Out of steam for love? Ask Jesus!

Lastly, there are those EGR (Extra Grace Required) people in your life. Usually these relationships are ones you didn't choose: a relative, ex-relative, in-law, ex-law, coworker, or neighbor. Even if you didn't choose a relationship with this person, he or she is now in your life and so you are responsible for how you choose to treat him or her.

Sometimes these people are difficult or hard to warm up to. They can be judgmental and argumentative or offer you all sorts of unfair and undeserved treatment.

4. Read 1 Thessalonians 4:1–11.

• With what kind of instruction does this passage begin?

• Beginning with verse 9, what is being spoken about?

• What are the key points of verses 11–12?

Lead a

Mind your

Work with

So that

You will not

With the difficult people in our lives, it is important that we concentrate on our own account-ability with the Lord. We need to be certain that we are living a life that pleases God. We must honor others with respectful and courteous behavior no matter how they treat us. The only way to do this is to fix our eyes on Jesus and depend solely on the Lord and His Spirit.

Father,
I need Your grace. I need Your love. I need Your strength to continue on in relationships that require my very last resource of emotional, physical, and spiritual energy. I thank You that each day, although I might be depleted, You are always full and ready to pour Your love through me. May I always seek Your strength and not live in the fickleness of my own. Amen.

 DAY FIVE: EXTRA GRACE REQUIRED IN REAL LIFE

In his book *On Being a Servant of God,* Warren Wiersbe says,

Difficult people and difficult circumstances can be used by the Spirit to help us grow and become more like Christ. However when these difficulties come, our tendency is to pray for deliverance instead of growth. When we do that we miss the opportunities God gives us to develop spiritual maturity. The devil wants to use problem people to tear you down, but the Spirit can use them as tools to build you up. The choice is yours.[2]

1. Read 1 Thessalonians 5:14–24.

This passage encourages you to seek another's best through the love of God. It actually says, *"make sure* that nobody pays back wrong for wrong, but always try to be kind to each other and to everyone else" (v. 15).

• Do you think this includes your EGR people? Journal your thoughts on this or write about a particular instance that comes to mind.

We live in a complex society. The family unit is not in one neat little package anymore. It was hard to live peacefully within the parameters of a traditional family unit, but now with the divorce rate what it is—we are a country filled with families that are all mixed up, bruised, and broken. We call this the "blended family."

You may be in a blended family unit, or you may be a single mother dealing with the remnant of divorce. Though this study is not on divorce, there is something worthy of comment here. You must include all the EGR people that are in your life in the mix of obeying Scripture. Your ex-husband is not excluded from God's command for you to love, and neither are any of your new blended family members.

I speak to Christian women frequently who refuse to have anything to do with their ex-spouses. This gives a double message to your children. Live to seek another's best, your children's best, and their children's best, by choosing to live at peace. You do not have to hang out with or be close friends with your ex-spouse—that portion of life is gone. But you do owe that person courteous respect and forgiveness. Remember the Lord and your children. Keep in mind the legacy you want to leave!

For many years I coordinated weddings for a local church. In this position I came across many families who were going through a big life event without the original family intact. It never ceased to amaze me how the Christians in these situations often acted. Glaring at each other, not speaking to each other, sniping each other with words, and passing messages through me, the wedding coordinator! How sad. What are we saying about our faith in these situations? Can God really give us His power and Spirit to rise above and pursue love?

2. Write out 1 Thessalonians 5:16–17.

• What does this verse say is God's will for you?

3. Read 1 Thessalonians 5:23–24 out loud.
• Write out 1 Thessalonians 5:24.

Make this verse of Scripture your prayer for this week. You and I can't live to seek another's best in our own strength. Life is filled with too many bumps and hurdles for that. We need God Himself, who is the God of peace, to work in us and through us.

Father,
Please empower me to be generous with Your love and encourage everyone
You have put in my life. May Your very best will be done in them, through
them, and for them. Amen!

Journal Page

- Journal a prayer asking God for help with a specific relationship.

KEY POINTS FROM LESSON 9

- Our human nature easily reverts to selfishness.
- Selfish actions and attitudes harm our relationships.
- All of our relationships are important—from home to the workplace.
- This world is not our home, so we are to live as those who are not of this world—living beyond ourselves.
- Daily relationships require love, care, and Spirit-infused living.
- God is working in us to teach us to love—it's His priority.
- We are to be courteous, caring, and considerate of others.
- We are to honor our parents.
- We are to love our children.
- Difficult people are part of life.
- God gives the extra grace required for relating in the real world.
- We are to live seeking another's best; this brings out the best in us and pleases God.

Living a New Pattern . . . The Lifestyle of Love

LESSON 10

We discover our hearts are finally free to love. They have become what the Creator intended them to be, places with the immense capacity to embrace. We may even hear ourselves saying, "Do you know there isn't anyone I can't love!" Then we will discover that God has done a real work in us.[1]

—KAREN BURTON MAINS

We often hear about lifestyle change in the realm of diet and health concerns. A woman has a heart attack, and suddenly she is thrown into the world of fat-less, salt-less living. She must embark on a lifestyle change if she is going to live. No more rich and calorie-laden eating for her! Years of living in that fashion have clogged her arteries and damaged her heart's ability to function. Her life depends on this change in lifestyle.

The same is true for all of us in the spiritual sense. No more rich and flesh-expensive actions for us, because years of living in the flesh have clogged our spiritual arteries and darkened our understanding of what it means to live in God's love. We suddenly may feel thrown into the world of slander-less, bitterness-less, and gossip-free living because the Great Physician told us that in order to live in the Spirit, we must put such ways of life behind us.

> Lifestyle: a way of life that reflects an individual's values.

Often our talk does not match our walk. Our way of life does not reflect our true heart-desired values. Learning to dwell in God's love will take some attitude adjusting, exercising of self-control (part of the fruit of the Spirit), lots of saturation in Scripture, as well as daily time in prayer. It begins with loving God with all of us—every bit of us. Then it moves on to understanding our value as God's created being and then into honoring others, because we understand that the love God has for us also extends to others.

Let's sum it all up by walking through Romans 12.

DAY ONE: PRESENTING OUR LIVES TO GOD

1. Read Romans 12:1. Paul here was urging believers in Rome to do something. What was it?

Offering your body is offering the whole of yourself to God. Paul tells these believers that this is what is reasonable for them to do. Before exhorting them to do this, he had just told them that everything comes from God—and through and to God are all things (Rom. 11:36). Now because of this, they are to present themselves to God. This is an act of *worship!*

Lifestyle change 1: Offer your life to God completely.

Have you offered all of yourself to God, or do you live on an insurance policy? Are you signed up for enough coverage to barely keep you from hell's flames, but not enough of Jesus to change your life and give you power to live?

2. Read Romans 12:3. Do you feel your attitudes are in line with the world you live in? Explain.

This world has a pattern, and that pattern is contrary to God's pattern. The only way we will be in God's good and perfect will is to turn from that pattern and embrace His Word and the pattern for living found there.

3. Read 2 Timothy 3:16.
• What does this verse say about God's Word?

• How can God's Word give your life a new pattern?

4. Write out Romans 12:2.

"Transformed by the renewing of your mind ..." What does that mean in real terms?

Transform means to turn completely inside out, to change the condition of, and to alter the function of our hearts and minds, which are full of only "us." We are sinful, and we need God's Spirit to make us new. Our arteries have been clogged with the debris of the culture we live in. The value system of our world has been building within us for many years and it has become ours. Some of us have taken on the value system of hypocrisy, and though we've lived in church all our lives, we haven't presented our wills to God. Our arteries are clogged from attitudes that are much like the Pharisees'. We need to be changed. How does that happen?

Renewing our minds means that when God's Word and its value system are put into our minds, we begin to think in a new and living way. We have insights we didn't previously have, and we respond to all of life differently. When we are in His Word, saturated in it, marinating in it, the flavor of who we are is transformed, and we are changed!

Father,
It is clear that Your will is for me to be surrendered to You—completely. I often surrender to the pressures or expectations of everything else around me. Help me to have spiritual boundaries—a boundary that puts You first in all things. To be aware of this on a daily basis will be a lifestyle change. I am trusting You. Amen.

Don't become so well-adjusted to your culture that you fit into it without even thinking. Instead, fix your attention on God. You'll be changed from the inside out. Readily recognize what he wants from you, and quickly respond to it. Unlike the culture around you, always dragging you down to its level of immaturity, God brings the best out of you, develops well-formed maturity in you (Rom. 12:2 MSG).

Day Two: Not of This World

1. Read Romans 12:3.

• What is this verse saying to you?

Lifestyle
change 2:
Turn away
from the
world's
philosophies.
}

• Does it seem like a contradiction to the message that God loves you and that you are of worth and value to Him? Explain.

Humility means that you recognize that God is God and you are not! You were created by Him and for Him; now you are to make your life subject to Him. Yes, He loves you with immeasurable love, but don't start exalting yourself. That is not God's way. God's way should lead you to an understanding of your true worth and to a desire to commit your life more fully to God as a result of that understanding.

God's way leads to confidence in your place in the world, but not to an overabundance of confidence, which would result in pride. Instead, your confidence will be seasoned with the reality check that every good and perfect gift comes from God, so everything good within you is from God. You will desire to submit to Him more because of His marvelous love!

2. Read Romans 12:4–5.

We are all part of one body. Now this is a lifestyle change in a world where people are islands to themselves, afraid to let other people in!

Lifestyle change 3: Be
changed by filling your
mind with God's way.
}

Our human bodies have many parts, and each part functions differently. Yet each part is important. So it is with the people of God. As Christians we belong to each other.

In this way we are like the various parts of a human body. Each part gets its meaning from the body as a whole, not the other way around. The body we're talking about is Christ's body of chosen people. Each of us finds our meaning and function as part of his body. But as a chopped-off finger or cut-off toe we wouldn't amount to much, would we? So since we find ourselves fashioned into all these excellently formed and marvelously functioning parts of Christ's body, let's just go ahead and be what we were made to be, without enviously or pridefully comparing with each other, or trying to be something we aren't.

—ROMANS 12:4–5 MSG

Lifestyle change 4: Humble yourself before God.

• What are your thoughts on Romans 12:4–5?

3. Read Romans 12:6–8. What is something you really like doing, something that comes naturally to you? What's it like for you to do that thing?

What you just described is probably one of your gifts. Sometimes it takes effort to uncover and recognize our gifts. But much of the time they are right in front of us. Quit trying to fit a round peg in a square hole. Stop trying to be anyone else. That is not God's way, and it leads to competition, envy, and jealousy. That's the opposite of living the lifestyle of love.

Recognize that God has a purpose for each person; have confidence in that part of His plan.

Father,
You have created me individually for Your use. I realize that I am to embrace what You have done for me as an individual and live for You. When I am focused on truth, I am confident and have no need to worry, fear, or compare. May that be my life. Amen.

Lifestyle change 5: Accept yourself and accept others as part of God's plan.

DAY THREE: DEVOTED TO THE TRUTH

1. Read Romans 12:9–10.

• According to these verses, what must love be?

Lifestyle change
6: Use your gifts
and don't compare
yourself with
other women.

}

• What are you to hate?

• To what are you to cling?

• To whom are you to be devoted?

• Whom are you to honor, and how?

Sincere:
genuine,
true, not
deceitful or
hypocritical.

}

Now isn't this interesting—we are to honor others above ourselves. This is in direct opposition to what the world says. This goes with lifestyle change 4, living in humility.

You are not in control of how another accepts or rejects your love. You might do nice things for some people who flatly ignore you and all that you do because of the anger in their own hearts. They may be jealous of you or threatened by you, so they can't honor you or be kind back to you. Just relax, give every relationship over to God. It is not the end of the world if someone doesn't like you or accept you. Unfair, maybe … but not the end of the world. You are responsible for your actions, not the actions of others.

2. Read Romans 12:11–13.

• What do you see here that you are to do?

> Lifestyle change 7: Love and honor others.

• How do you think you can keep your spiritual fervor?

I strongly urge you to memorize Scripture. Nothing will change your life more radically than putting the truth of God's Word in your mind. Stay with one theme or verse for more than a day. Soak it up, let it do its perfect work in you.

I can remember a time when I had lost all desire for anything spiritual. I had been completely let down by ministry and by Christians. My focus was all about *me* and who had let me down. I needed to redirect my focus. I got out the 3 x 5 cards, and I put on a sports watch. Every

> Lifestyle change 8: Be joyful and put your hope in God.

time that watch beeped, every thirty minutes, I would read a scripture from a selected few verses that I needed at the time. Before long I began to realize that people are just people like me, and people will always let me down. That is life. Christians are no exception. (That is a hard one, because we expect perfection out of Christians, don't we? How unfair!) My heart began to soften at the touch of God's Word, and once again my zeal for Jesus began to take root and come alive. And, again I could be

- joyful in hope,
- patient in affliction,
- faithful in prayer.

And with the attention and focus off me, I could once again share with God's people and be hospitable in heart and action.

Lifestyle change 9: Bless those who wrong you. Do not stoop to cursing them.

3. Read Romans 12:14. Write this one out!

Whoa! This is the hardest lifestyle change yet. I call this the torture verse, because it is torture to my flesh to obey this one. Yet when I do obey this verse, my oh my, do I ever get filled with the peace of God.

These aren't mere words for me, as I have had a few people in my life who have been life's most difficult challenge. Nothing I can do is right with them. I beat myself up for several years, trying to do it my way. Then one day I decided to turn these people over to God completely, and He took the burden. Now I make it a practice to pray daily for these people. I was in the habit of stooping to where they were—arguing, defending, being filled with anger. But by the grace of God, I now see He has a better way. Bless them!

Father,
I need to remember all that You have taught me about walking in love, in the Spirit, rather than in my selfish sinful nature. Make Your Word real to me, life to me, and wholeness for my relating to others. Amen.

 Day Four: Living a New Song

1. Read Romans 12:15–16. There are a lot of things here that are significant in a lifestyle change. Make a list of them.

Lifestyle change 10: Live in harmony with one another.

Now begin to use this list as your prayer list.

Again, you can only do your part. But your part can be huge in staying connected to God, at peace in your heart, and in giving you the ability to look in the mirror each morning. If someone doesn't want harmony, let it go. Don't make things worse by disregarding the directives in Scripture. Anger is usually the thing that gets us in trouble, but God has directions even for that.

Psalm 4:4–5 has been great for me. It tells me to take a time-out when I am angry. Instead of arguing and getting heated up, I am to be silent. Silent? Yes, silent before the Lord, offering a right sacrifice to Him, which is a heart toward God. When I silence everything within me, something wonderful happens to my heart. In a sane place, God can begin directing me in how to handle the person or problem that has made me so angry.

I am not saying to deny the anger, but to do as Scripture says: Take it to God. I cannot tell you how this one passage has changed my life! Really!

2. Read Romans 12:17–20.

• Again, write out these directives in a list.

• What are your thoughts about all these things that we are clearly being told should be part of our lifestyle?

> In your anger do not sin; when you are on your beds, search your hearts and be silent. Offer right sacrifices and trust in the LORD (Ps. 4:4–5).

These verses summarize the core of Christian living in the real world. When we love someone the way Christ loves us, we are willing to forgive and forsake our own self interest. By giving an enemy a drink we are not excusing the misdeed, but we are recognizing that person, loving, caring, and forgiving in spite of the misdeed toward us. This is the Jesus style!

Father,
Please send me Your Holy Spirit to help me come to grips with my anger, sort through what action I need to take, and live in harmony with others. I can't do this without You! Amen.

DAY FIVE: LOVE'S MIGHTY FIRE

1. Write out Romans 12:21. Memorize this one!

When something bad is happening in your life, don't let it overcome you, but go to God and let Him transform your attitude through the circumstance. If you have a lemon of an experience, then add sugar and make some drinkable lemonade out of it. It could be that God is using the sour to make your life sweeter!

In Philippians 4:4–8 Paul gave us a pattern for adding the sugar of the Spirit to a bad relationship or circumstance:

- Rejoice in the Lord.
- Do not be anxious.
- Pray.
- Thank God that He is in control.
- Receive His peace.
- Think about the good, dwell there.
- Receive some more of His peace.

Can you see how God's Word can be completely functional and practical when we break it down to digest it into our lives?

2. Now let's review all ten steps of living the lifestyle of love. Write down some things you have learned about each.

Offer your life to God completely.

Turn away from the world's philosophies.

Be changed by filling your mind with God's way.

Humble yourself before God.

Accept yourself and accept others as part of God's plan.

Use your gifts and don't compare yourself with other women.

Love and honor others.

Be joyful and put your hope in God.

Bless those who wrong you. Do not stoop to cursing them.

Live in harmony with one another.

Love ... burns like blazing fire,
like a mighty flame.
Many waters cannot quench love;
rivers cannot wash it away.

—SONG OF SONGS 8:6–7

Father,

Living in a new lifestyle requires change, and often I don't have the strength or desire to change. I see clearly from a study in Your Word that I am to live a lifestyle of love, thus changing my normal way of relating to others. I desire to live to please You and walk in Your Spirit. Thank You for Your Word and Your instruction on such practical, everyday things. I give my heart to You. Work in me. Amen.

Journal Page

- The aspects of the lifestyle of love that I most need to take action on are …

_____

_____

_____

_____

_____

_____

_____

_____

_____

_____

_____

_____

_____

_____

_____

_____

_____

_____

_____

_____

_____

_____

_____

_____

_____

KEY POINTS FROM LESSON 10

- God created us for His purpose and pleasure.
- Because He created us, we are to offer our lives to God completely.
- Because we are His, we are to turn away from the world's philosophies.
- *Agape* love is the supernatural love that resides in us because we have the Holy Spirit.
- *Agape* love is different from human love.
- We can be changed by filling our minds with God's way and depending on the Spirit's power.
- We are to humble ourselves before God daily—His mercies are new every morning.
- Accept yourself and others as part of God's plan.
- Use your gifts and don't compare yourself with other women.
- Love and honor others.
- Be joyful and put your hope in God.
- Bless those who wrong you. Do not stoop to cursing them.
- Live in harmony with one another.

Endnotes

INTRODUCTION

1 Joanne Wallace and Deanna Wallace, "Daily Prayer," *As Refreshing as Snow in the Hot Summertime* (Lincoln City, OR: Joanne Wallace Seminars, 2001), 68.

ONE: LIVING LOVE ... IN OUR DAILY CHOICES

1 Edward W. Goodrick and John R. Kohlenberger III, *NIV Exhaustive Concordance* (Grand Rapids, MI: Zondervan, 1990), 800–831.

2 C. S. Lewis, *The Four Loves* (New York: Harcourt Brace Jovanovich, 1960), 11.

3 Max Lucado, *Just Like Jesus* (Nashville: Word, 1998), 66.

4 Lucado, *Just Like Jesus*, 13–14.

TWO: LIVING LOVE ... AS GOD HAS LOVED US

1 *Roget's II: The New Thesaurus* (Boston: Houghton Mifflin, 1980).

2 Chuck Smith, *Living Water* (Eugene, OR: Harvest House, 1996), 13.

3 Smith, *Living Water*, 83.

4 Smith, *Living Water*, 85.

5 Taken from Debbie Alsdorf, *Deeper: Living in the Reality of God's Love* (Grand Rapids, MI: Revell, 2008).

FOUR: LIVING LOVE ... DESPITE OUR HURTS

1 Oswald Chambers, *Conformed to His Image* (Burlington, Ontario: Welch Publishing, 1985), 90.

2 Floyd McClung, Jr. (Seattle: YWAM Publishing, 1992), 28.

3 Henry Gariepy, *Portraits of Christ* (Grand Rapids, MI: Revell, 1974), quoted by Kirkie Morrissey, *In His Name* (Colorado Springs: NavPress, 1984), 83.

FIVE: LIVING FORGIVENESS ... TRUE FREEDOM

1 Karen Burton Mains, *The Key to an Open Heart* (Colorado Springs: David C. Cook, 1979), 20.

2 Steve Bearden, as quoted by Joanne Wallace, *Starting Over Again* (Nashville: Thomas Nelson, 1991), 75.

3 Dr. Henry Cloud and Dr. John Townsend, *12 Christian Beliefs That Can Drive You Crazy* (Grand Rapids, MI: Zondervan, 1995), 75.

SIX: LIVING MERCY ... AS HE IS MERCIFUL

1 Tim Hansel, *Keep on Dancin'* (Colorado Springs: Chariot Victor, 1995), 312.

SEVEN: LIVING KINDNESS ... THE REFRESHED LIFE

1 *God's Little Devotional Book* (Tulsa, OK: Honor Books, 1995), 8.

2 Charles Stanley, *Living in the Power of the Holy Spirit* (Nashville: Thomas Nelson, 2005), 46–47.

3 Max Lucado, *Just Like Jesus*, 67.

EIGHT: LIVING REAL . . . THE PRACTICAL SIDE OF LOVE

1 L. B. Cowman, *Streams in the Desert* (Grand Rapids, MI: Zondervan, 1997), 92.

2 Ruth Harms Calkin, *Lord, Could You Hurry a Little?* (Wheaton, IL: Tyndale, 1983), 79.

NINE: LIVING UNSELFISHLY . . . SEEKING ANOTHER'S BEST

1 Hansel, *Keep on Dancin'*, 354.

2 Warren Wiersbe, *On Being a Servant of God* (Nashville: Thomas Nelson, 1993), 16–17.

TEN: LIVING A NEW PATTERN . . . THE LIFESTYLE OF LOVE

1 Karen Burton Mains, *The Key to an Open Heart*, 20.

Reasonable care has been taken to trace ownership of the materials quoted in this book and to obtain permission to use copyrighted materials when necessary.